ACTS OF
RESISTANCE

*A Freedom Rider Looks Back
On the Civil Rights Movement*

Judith Frieze Wright

ACTS OF RESISTANCE

A Freedom Rider Looks Back
On the Civil Rights Movement

Acts of Resistance: A Freedom Rider Looks Back on the Civil Rights Movement

By Judith Frieze Wright
Published by Apple Bay Publishing

ISBN 9781793370334
Library of Congress Control Number 2019900972

Jacket design: Christa Johnson.
Cover photo (Public Domain).
Book and website design: Jalina Mhyana and Catherine Parnell.

Photograph of the author by Jan Weinshanker.

For Nina, Luke, Erik,
Griffin and Skye
and in memory of my parents,
Philip and Bernice Frieze

Harlem

What happens to a dream deferred?

Does it dry up
Like a raisin in the sun?
Or fester like a sore—
And then run?
Does it stink like rotten meat?
Or crust and sugar over—
Like a syrupy sweet?

Maybe it just sags
Like a heavy load

Or does it explode?

Langston Hughes, excerpt from *Harlem* [2]

PROLOGUE

In the spring of 1999 I walked up the dim narrow stairs to my third-floor attic and sat cross-legged on the rough wood floor. A dusty beam of morning light came in through the small window in the attic of the house where Sib and I had brought up our two children, Nina and Luke. They were both off on their own now. It was time Sib and I moved on as well, and before we left for our new home, the clutter of the last twenty-two years had to be confronted, sorted, and for the most part put out on the sidewalk.

The low wood walls and sloping ceiling were dark, unfinished, and as rough as the floor; the shadowy shelves were crammed with unappreciated gifts and cardboard boxes full of memories. I'd forgotten, but it was now clear that I had saved every treasured childhood drawing and scrap of writing that Nina and Luke had ever produced. Tears for our past times together blurred my sight as I tried to pick out the most memorable items and save one carton for each of them, achingly putting the rest aside to throw away. I came across some other things too: old love letters from a boyfriend I had before I met Sib. These went in the "dispose of" pile as well.

There were only a couple of cartons left. I yanked one down, and like the others it fell before me with a dusty thud. Rummaging through it, I came upon a bunch of pale blue papers folded into a rectangular shape not more than two inches wide and six inches long. The papers were stiff with age, and made a crisp, crackly sound as I carefully peeled them apart. What once had to have been words were now no more than faded and blurred watermarks and blotches. Whatever message these pages contained, it was gone forever.

If the words were just faded beyond recognition the papers probably would have gone straight to the trash pile; what had me puzzled was why they were so blurred. Then, with a jolt, it came back to me that this packet was the diary I had kept for six weeks in the summer of 1961, while in the maximum security unit at Mississippi's Parchman State Penitentiary following my arrest for taking part in the Freedom Rides during the Civil Rights Movement. Our goal was to have hundreds of people, both black and white, arrested and jailed in order to bring attention to the unlawful segregation of interstate travel in the Deep South.

Once released, I had returned home suffering from asthma and malnutrition. My always caring mother, trying to make things normal for me again, had put all my filthy traveling and prison clothes in the wash. I was probably upstairs taking a shower, but whatever I was doing I hadn't yet told her that just before I left my cell, I had folded the diary and carefully hidden it in the hem of the gray and white striped seersucker skirt I'd worn South and which was given back to me to wear home. When the dripping and meaningless pages were retrieved, my devastated mother hid her face in her hands and came close to weeping. It was impossible to do anything but comfort her.

In the attic, all those years later, I kept looking at the diary hoping that what was now a fragment of history, and at the very least would have triggered a rush of memories, would magically reappear on the page. They didn't, of course, and I was left wondering whether my memories of that time would be as fragile and lost as the washed-out words in the diary.

◊

What were the Freedom Rides?

Although the Supreme Court had ruled in 1946 that segregated interstate travel was prohibited, the Southern states, as part of their ongoing stance against any kind of integration, ignored these rulings. In May of 1961 the first Freedom Ride occurred: an integrated group of Civil Rights activists decided to challenge this noncompliance by traveling together through the South by bus. The first bus was attacked and burned. Nobody was killed, but despite beatings and jailings of the riders, more buses of activists continued to arrive in the South. Eventually over 400 riders were jailed. Publicity about this caused widespread concern around the country, and in September of 1961, the Interstate Commerce Commission issued orders that the Supreme Court decision against segregation in interstate travel must be obeyed. Soon all travelers could sit wherever they pleased on buses and trains. "Colored" and "White" signs came down over terminal water fountains and rest rooms; waiting rooms and lunch counters became integrated.

The victory achieved by Freedom Riders helped to inspire the subsequent struggle for other equal rights, especially voting rights, for African Americans in the South.

◊

As history brings changes, language often is modified in response. The words used to identify race are a prime example of this, and there will most likely be more changes in the future. But for now, in this memoir, I use five terms to describe African Americans: *black, negro, colored, n——,* and *African American.*

In the sixties *black* was the respectful and common word used to describe African Americans. Therefore, I have used it while telling the story of my experiences during that time. Before *black* came into conventional usage, the words *negro* or *colored* were most often used and they appear, although minimally, in this memoir.

In some places you will see *n——,* which indicates the use of a completely unacceptable word. In this book, the word comes out of the mouth of an angry, demeaning, and bigoted individual. It was of common usage in those times by ignorant, intolerant, and racist people. I use African American when writing in the present tense.

TABLE OF CONTENTS

Part One

THE ROAD TO PARCHMAN
STATE PENITENTIARY

ONE
FINDING MY MORAL COMPASS

I'm on my way to freedom land
I'm on my way to freedom land
I'm on my way to freedom land
Great God, I'm on my way

Verse from "I'm on My Way to Freedom Land."
Based on a spiritual.

In the 1950s, when I was a teenager, my parents gave me *Exodus* by Leon Uris as a birthday gift. The story—about the struggle of the Jewish people to establish a homeland in what was then Palestine—drew me into another world far from my own life. It also touched off a longing in me for a life of significance, an opportunity to help make the world a better place.

My parents, my brother Michael, and I lived in Newton, a comfortable middle-class, predominantly white suburb of

Boston. My life was easy and happy, but I already knew that it wasn't the life for me. I wanted something more. I wanted my life to be important, and nothing in my experience so far could compare with the drama and adventure of *Exodus.* My profound reaction to the book was not so much because I'm Jewish, but because the characters were devoting their lives to something they passionately believed in. I was beginning to understand the contrast between my tranquil life and the terrible wrongs that were ongoing throughout the world. Like many young people of that time, restless and increasingly alienated from the blandness of the 1950s, I longed to make my life meaningful: it was an ideological vision, and it remained a treasured fantasy of my Newton years. I knew I wanted a different life.

When I arrived at Smith College in 1957, officially sanctioned segregation was in full force in the South. The horribly brutal and humiliating caste system that began with the first slaves stolen from Africa was still in evidence. Black people were not allowed to sit at lunch counters where white people ate. Nor could they drink out of the same water fountains, use the same rest rooms, or ride anywhere but in the back of buses. For the most part, they couldn't get any but the most menial jobs. Most critically, they were prevented from voting, which meant that none of these shameful practices could be changed democratically by their vote.

As late as the 1950s, lynching still occurred, the most well-known of which was that of a fourteen-year-old boy from Chicago who came to Mississippi to visit relatives. Emmett Till had allegedly whistled at a white woman in the grocery store, and two nights later he was abducted from the home of his relatives. He was taken into a barn, tortured, mutilated, and finally beaten to death. His body was thrown into the Tallahatchie River, where it was found several days later. The woman's husband and his half-brother were arrested for the crime, but to no one's surprise, they were quickly acquitted.

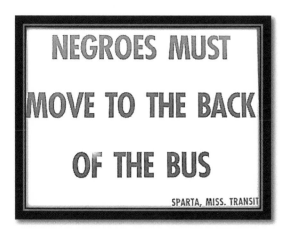

Signs like this appeared all over the South.

Now, protected by the doctrine of double jeopardy from being retried, both men readily admitted, perhaps even bragged that they were the killers. Completing the story of what really happened, in 2008 the woman acknowledged that she had made up her version of the encounter with Till.

When Emmett Till's body was sent home Mamie Bradley (his mother) insisted on an open casket at the funeral. She wanted the world to see what had been done to her only child, and she made sure that a photograph of him in his coffin, showing his crushed and disfigured body, was published in black newspapers all over the country. She knew that unless this happened, the murder of her beloved son would go virtually unnoticed. The widespread and outraged reaction to the lynching of a fourteen-year-old child, the quick acquittal of his killers, and their subsequent acknowledgement of guilt is considered by many to be the decisive event that gave birth to the modern Civil Rights Movement.

Emmett Till with his mother, Mamie Till Bradley Mobley

(ca. 1953-1955).

Thankfully, incidents like this were not as horrifically commonplace at that time as they once were. Living in the North, my knowledge of these kinds of practices and events was more limited than it should have been, as I had never been personally exposed to overt and life-threatening acts of racism. But that was about to change.

I remember a moment in my college dorm room, sitting on my blue quilt, *The Boston Globe* spread out before me. The sun coming through the trees outside my small window made light patches on the pages of the paper. It was 1960 and the start of my senior year. The paper's front page was given over to the latest news—upsetting and exciting—about a few courageous black students asking to be served at segregated lunch counters in Greensboro, North Carolina. The sit-ins had begun.

Jackson, Mississippi: Woolworth Lunch Counter Sit-In, 1963.

My eyes fixed on the horrifying images of the students and their white supporters, neatly dressed and self-possessed, while groups of snarling white bullies dumped food on their heads and dragged them off their stools to be beaten. The end of these episodes was always the same: those asking for service quietly and nonviolently were arrested for disturbing the peace while the bullies, still jeering, were disbursed by the police.

Every day I waited for the paper to arrive, hungry to read about the latest outrage inflicted upon those participating in this new form of political action.

Although I had grown up in an area that was practically all white, I did get to know quite a few black people. Walter Haywood, who worked with my father, wasn't a whole lot older than I was during my high school years. He sometimes came to visit us, and we got to know his family and some of his friends and neighbors. I remember Ruth Turner and her family, Rose and Joe Williamson, and others with whom I felt a warm connection over many years.

I was certainly aware of racism, but rarely talked about race or about what was going on in the South when I was with them. I hadn't really comprehended the enormity and brutality of racial segregation before all this news about Emmet Till and the sit-ins, so the stories in the paper truly hit me hard.

Later that school year, in the spring of 1961, I sat glued to the TV in the large living room of my dormitory watching reports of the first Freedom Rides. An integrated group of brave young people had taken a bus across the Deep South in order to confront the segregation of bus stations and other facilities engaged in interstate travel. Although this was their immediate goal, it was clear to me that their true purpose was to lift the shame of segregation out from under the blanket of national neglect and into the light for all to see. Their plan was to get arrested and refuse bail. They did not doubt that many others would follow suit and they were certain the publicity caused by so many young people in jail would wake up the country and force the federal government, which had exclusive jurisdiction over interstate commerce, to end segregation of buses and related facilities. I envied these people. I wanted to be like them. I wanted to be part of something so important.

That first ride was met with not-unexpected violence: in Anniston, Alabama a mob stopped the bus and set it on fire. They beat the frightened riders as they attempted to escape into the surrounding area.

But the rides did not stop.

In Birmingham, riders were beaten upon arrival by hundreds of angry Southerners brandishing axe handles and pipes. Eugene "Bull" Connor, the Commissioner of Public Safety, whose job included oversight of the Birmingham police department, was notorious for enforcing segregation, sometimes with extreme cruelty and indifference to the civil rights of black citizens. He was well known as the violent personification of the Southern white power structure. At the Birmingham Trailways station, Bull Connor ordered the police to stand by for the first 15 minutes—long enough to give the mob the time it needed to break bones and leave people unconscious. When that job was done, the police moved in and arrested the Freedom Riders.

And still the rides continued.

I couldn't stop thinking about these people and how deeply they believed in what they were doing. Despite the inevitable consequences, including beatings and prison, they were not going to falter. I saw clearly that people like Bull Connor and other racists needed to be stopped and that activism by protestors was attracting our whole country's attention to the problem. By the end of the school year I had made up my mind to join the Freedom Riders.

After graduating I went home and told my parents I wanted to go South to be part of what was happening. They were frightened, as any parent would be.

"You can't really do this, Judy. What if your asthma gets bad?" implored my mother.

I could only reply, "I'll be fine. Please don't worry," which must have sounded totally naïve to them, and not at all reassuring.

My father was just as distraught as my mother. Lowering his head and shaking it with worry, he pleaded with me to be reasonable, to participate in the growing protest in some other way.

I can only imagine how hard my decision was for my parents, two people who had always supported me, but now were in the position of having to push hard against something I really wanted to do and that they, too, felt was morally just. Finally, we agreed on a compromise. I would go see our beloved friend and family doctor, Chick Portner, and ask his advice about my asthma and this trip. My parents agreed that they would drop their objections if Chick thought it was reasonable for me to go. I told Chick how strongly I felt about participating in this, and I still remember his response: "Judy, your parents can't be everything to you. You should go." As promised, my mother and father swallowed hard and gave me their full support. This was the first time I had stood up so strongly against the wishes of my parents. It was an uncomfortable situation, but I was determined.

A few days later, I packed a small bag for what I thought would be a quick interview, casually said goodbye to my mother and father, and headed for New York to volunteer at CORE (the Congress of Racial Equality) where, according to the newspapers, the rides were being organized. I expected to stay only overnight and return home again to await word on when it would be my turn to leave for the South.

I boarded a bus in Boston, and sitting in an isolated seat, began to think about the important journey that awaited me. My throat was tight. Was I ready? Would I be strong enough? Would the person I spoke to in New York believe that I was capable of being part of what was then being called the "Movement," a term that covered the many struggles going on against segregation in the South?

TWO
GETTING ON THE BUS

If you miss me at the back of the bus
And you can't find me nowhere
Come on over to the front of the bus
I'll be ridin' up there.

Verse from "If You Miss Me from the Back of the Bus"
by Carver Neblettt (aka Seku Neblett).

June 1961

CORE was located in a small second floor office in a modest brick building across from a tiny city park. After walking up the narrow stairway and timidly introducing myself, I sat down at a simple green table across from a black man who introduced himself as Larry. He smiled at me and gently said, "I understand that you're here because you want to go South and join the Freedom Rides."

For lack of any better response, I managed to mumble, "Yes, that's right."

"But what brought you to this point?"

"I've been reading about what's going on and I'm really upset. I've been hoping to do something like this for a very long time. I know you need people."

"Do you have any idea what you're getting into?" This time he was a bit less gentle.

"Only what I've read in the papers." My hands were damp. I was trying hard to sound more sure of myself than I felt.

"I want to tell you something," Larry continued. "This is no easy thing to do, there's a good possibility you'll face violence. Even if you manage to avoid that, all the Freedom Riders are being arrested and going to jail now. Do you know what jail in Mississippi is like, especially for a 'n—— lover' like you? You will be under the thumb of people who hate you." Larry's voice became almost scolding. "Among other things, Judy, you might be beaten. You could be put in a cell by yourself and for how long I'm not exactly sure. People have been thrown in jail with serious injuries, but their complaints have never reached anyone who could help. Your jailers will make things as tough on you as they possibly can."

Larry paused to let his words sink in. My head had slipped into a foggy escape mode as he painted this horrid picture. It was as if my determination had built a barrier against hearing anything that might persuade me not to go South. Though Larry's words were unsettling, the reality seemed very far away—far enough away for me to finally say, "I can do it."

"You're sure?"

"Yes."

I then found out I would be going South in two days. Taking a deep breath, I called my parents to let them know I would be leaving much sooner than expected and I wouldn't be able to come home first. I wished that I had given them bigger hugs when I said goodbye that morning.

The next day I went through nonviolence training. I learned how to roll myself up in a ball with my arms bent to cover my head for protection. The importance of remaining polite and nonviolent no matter what was happening was drilled into me. If the police took me away, I was to be uncooperative by going "limp" and forcing the police to carry or drag me. (Later I heard this called "putting the limp on 'em.") Everyone involved was to follow Gandhi's practice of Jail-No-Bail.

I left for Atlanta the following morning to meet up with the eight other people who would be traveling with me from Atlanta through Alabama—and then into the very heart of segregation: Mississippi.

When I arrived in Atlanta, I met the Freedom Riders in my group: four black men, one black woman, one white man, and three white women. Sissy, one of the white women, had a delicate build, short blonde hair, huge glasses, and faultless skin. She was about twenty and had grown up in Georgia. "I have to do this," she quietly explained, "because I can't bear it that people think that all Southerners are like the ones they see on the television news."

Reverend Wyatt Tee Walker and his wife Theresa, both black, were in the group. Wyatt was the executive director of the Southern Christian Leadership Conference, Martin Luther King Jr.'s organization, and was our group leader. Although he was a minister, he told us that earlier in his life he used to carry a gun, just waiting for some racist to confront him so he could shoot him. Then he met Martin Luther King Jr. and was convinced to "put up his gun." His wife Theresa, already a Civil Rights activist, was there right by his side.

Mimi Feinberg, white, was a college student from New York. She had experience picketing local businesses to support the sit-ins in the South and seemed to me to be far more politically sophisticated than I was. She was close to my age, and later we ended up sharing a cell for part of our time in Parchman State Penitentiary.

The only white man in our group was Henry Schwartzchild, also from New York. Henry had taken part in the sit-ins, and would later work closely with Martin Luther King, attending events where they would both speak.

The other three men in our group were Samuel Nash, Melvin White, and Reverend Leon Smith. So much time has gone by that I don't remember any specifics about these last three men, but I do know they were as courageous and committed to what we were doing as any of the rest of us.

The time came to buy our tickets for the Trailways bus that would take us on our protest ride through the Deep South. As I laid out my money, I was very aware that I was buying a ticket to take part in the struggle for civil rights. This was my first step . . . buying a ticket to jail. But even then, I felt no fear. Being young and far too innocent, I thought I was totally invulnerable. The black people in our group had no such illusions.

When we settled on the bus out of Atlanta, grouped together toward the middle, quiet overtook us. Other passengers, white ones, gave our integrated group hostile looks and stayed as far from us as they could. A few of them averted their eyes altogether. Some of them had probably seen the stories about Anniston and Birmingham on TV and were both angry and frightened by what might happen this time. Black passengers who were not part of our group had all moved to their "proper" place in the back.

After putting my small bag in the rack above my head, I looked around. It was a large bus with spacious seats covered in red fabric. The air was hot and smelled faintly of gasoline. I heard the motor rev up, and then the bus jerked, backed away from the station, and started on its journey through Georgia. We chatted casually, although it was obvious that I wasn't the only one feeling a bit queasy. We faced straight ahead, our eyes darting from side to side.

When we entered Alabama, Wyatt faced our small group, still isolated from the ordinary passengers by the tiers of empty seats in front and in back of us, and in a low voice began his instructions. We were going to arrive that day in Birmingham, Alabama, the stronghold of Bull Connor.

First Wyatt looked at each one of us straight on. "If there's a mob there," he warned, "all of us must surround Henry. The most hated among us is a white man who joins the Civil Rights struggle—they'll go for him first. Next will come the black man, then the black woman, and last of all, the white woman. If you're a white woman and you're being attacked, scream as loud as you can and maybe, just maybe, they'll have pity on you."

Then he reminded us of our commitment to nonviolence.

I felt our group descend into fear, akin to the alarm my parents must have felt when I told them about my plans. I suddenly wondered whether I could handle any of this. Would I even be able to scream? How would they hurt me? What would the pain feel like? I was on total high-alert. My clothes felt damp, and for the first time I was aware of the odor of many tense people crammed together in the heat. Birmingham was getting closer, and silence again fell over all of us, protestors and ordinary travelers alike.

As our bus approached the Birmingham Trailways station, we craned our necks to see if a mob was gathering. But when we finally came to a stop the tenseness in our bodies and our minds seeped away; there was no angry crowd. Instead, there were police whose instructions, it quickly became clear, were to make sure that we passed through Birmingham safely.

Later, I found out that this change in reception tactics was due to pressure from the United States Justice Department, which wanted to end all the horrific publicity about the rides so that the Civil Rights organizations might move on to a less confrontational strategy, and to the realization by Birmingham city officials that they'd more readily get back to their own way of doing things if the "outside agitation" withered away for lack of such publicity.

Police held back scornful and sneering white onlookers and escorted us into the bus station. Eventually each of us was sent off to spend the night with a courageous black family risking its own safety and anonymity to support the Civil Rights Movement. If any of these host families were identified, dismissal from jobs, harassment, and even beatings could be the price they would pay. To help avoid these dangers, rather than having the families come to the bus station to pick up the Freedom Riders, we were taken to the homes of the volunteer families by other Civil Rights workers.

That evening all eight of us, as well as our host families, met at a black church. It was a modest, freshly-painted white building, more the size of a large house than the places of worship I was used to. There were no broad and imposing steps into the building, no pillars, no stained glass windows; yet it stood out unmistakably from the very modest and somewhat run-down houses in the surrounding neighborhood. As my host family and I neared the church, I heard the distant sounds of singing and clapping, louder and louder as we got closer.

When we opened the door, the sound burst out in all its glory. The other Freedom Riders had arrived, as had many local black people, there to lend whatever support they could. The indoor space was plain and set up like a meeting room with simple folding chairs. There was a foot high-rise in the wooden floor across the front where the preacher could stand during a service.

*A group of Civil Rights workers share their
strength by singing "We Shall Overcome" (1964).*

Blacks and whites stood together in a tight circle, arms crossed in front and hands clasping the person on each side. Their shining faces were raised as they sang the songs of the Movement. I didn't yet know most of these anthems, but Mimi, who had already arrived, seemed totally at home singing "Oh Freedom," "We Shall Overcome," and "Hallelujah I'm a Travelin'."

I felt intensely awkward and totally out of place—a newcomer entering a world where everyone but me knew one other and knew what to do. They were already immersed in something very momentous, something that I was still at the very edge of. At the same time my whole being was excited and lifted high by what I heard and saw. After a while the welcoming looks on people's faces overcame my self-consciousness—and I joined the circle.

As time went on I came to appreciate the important role that music played in the Movement. It was the emotional bedrock of our political activity. It held us all together and gave us both courage and an inspired vision of how things could be. We heard the music of the Movement everywhere: at demonstrations, in jails, and at meetings. We joined hands and sang the Movement's songs whenever we needed to share our joy and determination, as well as our fear.

Being with everyone that night was also my first introduction to the dynamic role played by the churches in the Civil Rights protests and in Southern black culture as a whole. The church was the backbone of communities from which so many people joined in the struggle, gave their time and risked their lives. Three years later, when I worked in Meridian,

Mississippi, I would get to know and work with many committed and brave church members, especially the women, without whom we would have been strangers in the community.

The next morning we were back on the bus. I was a bit more relaxed, as we no longer had to face the danger we had feared was awaiting us in Birmingham. It was to be a long day, and as the bus made its way through Alabama and eventually into Mississippi, an unfamiliar landscape slid by my window. Tiny, dilapidated and isolated shacks were set far back from the road on barren brown fields, looking so alone and vulnerable. Shingles were missing; tattered and patched roofs sagged. Small black children, bare-footed and dressed in faded clothes, played outside in the dull red dirt, while here and there an adult sat on a crooked porch or hung laundry on a rope strung between a shack and a slanted pole in the ground. Occasionally an ancient car or battered bicycle stood nearby, but no driveways or paths led from the road to these homes. Monotonous dry earth colors dominated the view like an old sepia photograph against the blue sky. For the first time I really got it that not much had changed since the days of slavery and the servitude of blacks under the tenant farmer system that followed.

As we rode along I was glued to the window. Soon we would reach Jackson, Mississippi, where I knew I would be arrested.

When we arrived at the Trailways station in Jackson, our fellow passengers scrambled off the bus before any trouble started. Stiff from the long ride, I got out of my seat, grabbed my few possessions, and staying as close to the others in our group as I could, made my way into the white waiting room. Though I knew there would be very difficult times ahead, I was aware of how lucky we were to have safely arrived at the end of our ride.

As we walked together into the clean and bright white waiting room, I realized we were not alone. Several white people stood or sat watching us at a distance. They knew as well as we did what was about to happen. Most of them were silent but clearly gloating.

By now, the arrest of Freedom Riders had become almost routine. We stood quietly as a policeman approached us and introduced himself as Captain Ray. He had a big belly and was wearing a gray uniform, a cowboy-style hat, and big black leather boots. "Are y'all gonna move on and move out of this here station?" he sternly asked. Wyatt politely answered, "No sir. We have a right to be here."

Captain Ray repeated, "I'm askin' again. Are y'all gonna move on and move out of this here station?"

When Wyatt again declined, Captain Ray announced, "Then ya'll are under arrest."

Part of me was relieved at that moment. I had known that this would happen, and that it was part of what needed to happen in order to challenge the indifference of most white Americans to the evils of segregation and to force an opening through the wall of inattention that hid what was really going on in the South. And though I didn't know what the next days and weeks would bring, I was glad that this phase, too, was over.

A strange, almost dreamlike sequence followed. Captain Ray, swaying from side to side as he put one foot in front of the other, led us out into the street through scattered onlookers. Some were just curious, some smirked and some howled, shaking their fists at us and yelling "n—— lovers" or "Go back where you belong."

Freedom Riders in a paddy wagon on their way to jail after being arrested in Jackson, Mississippi on June 2, 1961.

A large black police van, or "paddy wagon," waited. I climbed in with the others, and stuffing my belongings under one of the hard metal benches that ran along each side, sat down crammed between Mimi and Theresa. The door closed with a harsh thud, and we were left in the scant and dreary light coming in through the small metal barred windows. The air was hot and stuffy. Though my body was tense and my throat dry, I smiled to myself as I realized that we had achieved at least one small victory: the paddy wagon was integrated.

It was only a short ride to the police station, where a uniformed policeman brought us out into the bright sunlight and then took us indoors. I was led into a side room where I stood obediently at a high counter while a policeman took each of my fingers separately, pressed its tip into an ink pad, and then pressed it again onto a sheet of paper divided into one section for each fingerprint. Then he told me to step back and two mug shots were taken, one facing forward, and one in profile. After each of us had been processed, we were taken to the Hinds County jail, where our belongings were impounded.

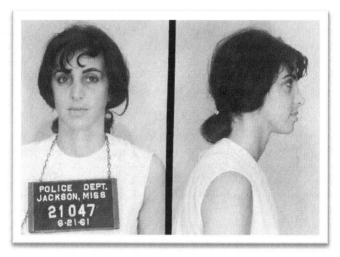

My mug shot, taken June 21, 1961.

Once there, our group was split up for the first time as the men were led away. Then the black women were taken off in one direction while Sissy, Mimi, and I were taken in another, through some barred doors, and then further down a corridor. As we neared our destination I could hear high-spirited voices singing "Oh, Freedom," and my own spirits lifted. I was about to meet new comrades and enter into a solidarity which would protect me, ease my fears, and take me one step further into the larger Movement.

The cell, which measured about twelve by sixteen feet, was meant for occasional arrests, but now held about twenty white women. Old dirty mattresses leaned against the walls: at night they would be placed on the floor, two for every three people. Tiny barred windows were set high above our heads, and steel bars along the front of the cell separated us from the corridor. Toward one wall, on a slightly elevated platform, stood a single toilet, a throne of humiliation. When I first saw it I had to look away in horror and dread of when I would have to use it. There also was a small sink which we all used to keep ourselves as clean as possible . . . and that was it.

We spent our time politely and nonviolently dealing with the circumstances as best we could. Sometimes we sang, sometimes we just chatted, trying to get to know each other better. We managed what little exercise we could in the cramped space.

The day after our arrival, our cell door clanged open as a policeman came to escort Mimi, Sissy, and me into a small, well-lit but sterile courtroom. There, sitting in a section off to the side and near a corner, were the other Freedom Riders from our bus. A magistrate sitting behind a large desk seemed impatient for us to take our places quickly. Instead of being charged with breaking the unlawful rules of segregation, we were charged with "Breach of Peace." I listened without surprise to the words of the lawyer for the state who spoke of us as outside agitators and troublemakers. Then our lawyer argued that segregation of interstate travel and facilities was against the law, and that we had remained peaceful in attempting to assert our rights. The arguments over, the magistrate, in a voice almost bored and totally devoid of emotion, found us all "guilty as charged."

We were each fined $200 and sentenced to four months in prison. I honestly wasn't surprised by the verdict, never having expected anything else.

Under Mississippi law we had forty days to appeal our sentences, which would result in our release pending the next stage of proceedings. The plan was for each of us to spend thirty-nine days in prison, then appeal and walk out. CORE was banking on its strategy of Jail-No-Bail to put hundreds of people behind bars, clog the system, generate a huge amount of publicity, and cause enough of a nationwide protest to either compel Mississippi to end the segregation of its interstate travel facilities, or force the federal government to intervene and do the job itself. I felt privileged and I welcomed being one of that number.

We all gave each other comforting looks as we were led out of the courtroom and back to our segregated cells. The magistrate's decision made us convicted criminals until the U.S. Supreme Court reversed our guilty verdicts in 1965.

The next day one of the women whose mother had sent her a box of stationery kindly offered me a few pages and a pen. I took these things gratefully and began keeping my ill-fated diary. I wrote about arriving at the county jail, about the songs we sang, about living in a small cell with twenty women, one toilet, one sink, and two-thirds of a mattress, and how my spirits nevertheless soared. I was finally part of something of great consequence.

It wasn't more than a few days later when a guard stood outside our bars and announced, "Get yourselves together, girls, you're going to Parchman State Penitentiary." I remember gripping the edge of the mattress and swallowing hard. The brutal practices at Parchman Farm (the informal name for the Mississippi State Penitentiary) were well known.

A view of the entrance to Parchman State Penitentiary.
This photo was taken in 2011 when many Freedom Riders
returned for a 50th anniversary visit.

We were given back our belongings and led outside where a small bus was waiting. I didn't even notice the few moments of fresh air before I climbed the three steps into the oppressive heat of the bus and sat down, my hands cold and my chest tight.

The ride from Jackson to Parchman took about four hours, and we spent a good part of it singing freedom songs. It's what we always did when we were afraid. The crowded cityscape of Jackson slowly gave way to middle-class homes with well-tended lawns and then suddenly to run-down shacks on dirt patches. We had arrived in the real heart of segregation and oppression: the Mississippi Delta. At the end of the trip when our bus drove under a huge archway boldly proclaiming "Mississippi State Penitentiary" across the top, I experienced both a sinking feeling and a swell of curiosity.

THREE

LIVING BEHIND BARS

Paul and Silas bound in jail
Ain't nobody gonna' pay their bail.
Keep your eyes on the prize,
Hold on. Hold on.

Verse from "Keep Your Eyes on the Prize."
Based on a spiritual.

June-July 1961

The road inside led us past several institutional looking buildings before the bus pulled up at the entrance to a wide cement path lined on both sides with a high fence topped with barbed wire that curved inward and over us like huge claws. We climbed down from the bus and numbly followed a guard toward the building at the end of the walkway. We were in front of the maximum security unit, a square brick structure with a large entrance made of metal bars. There were no visible windows.

Freedom Riders visited the maximum security unit at
Parchman in 2011 on the 50th anniversary of the protest.

After all of us were escorted into the very ominous looking building, the men and women were separated. Led by a trusty (a prisoner who was given responsibility to watch over other prisoners), the women followed each other down a flight of steep metal stairs running along a dull gray cement wall. At the bottom we found ourselves at the beginning of a long sterile corridor on one side of which was an equally long row of heavily barred cells. This was one of Parchman's maximum security units, where we were to be incarcerated, not only to intimidate us but to keep us out of reach of other prisoners who, if they were white, might attack us. With so much national publicity about Freedom Rides saturating the country, a brutal beating was the last thing the state of Mississippi wanted.

Though I knew something like this was coming, the reality of it shocked me. John F. Kennedy Jr., who was our President at that time, had been a bit slow to support the Freedom Rides, but had changed his mind and was now on the side of the protesters. I remember having a fleeting hope that "Kennedy won't let this happen," wishing away what I saw in front of me. What kind of world was it that would force us into a dark situation like this? On the other hand, the Freedom Riders' hopes were being fulfilled. The cell block was filling up and hundreds more Riders were on their way.

For those at Parchman watching this happen, I'm sure there were two conflicting reactions: the African American trusties, while remaining expressionless, might well have been inwardly cheering us, while the white prison personnel were clearly enjoying the incarceration of people who they considered decadent outside agitators.

Before anything else, each woman, one by one, was taken into a small bare room and searched. When it was my turn, a stolid uniformed woman with a severe expression ordered me to take off all my clothes below the waist and to then lie down on the gurney beside me. Horrified, I watched her pull on a used blue rubber glove and dip it in a bucket of Lysol before performing an internal search. My whole body clamped down as I closed my eyes tightly and clenched my teeth to endure it as best I could. When it was over, a trusty took my clothes and gave me my striped prison garments. I got dressed and rejoined the other women. All of us wore stunned expressions.

Next, accompanied by cheers and singing from the women prisoners who were already there, we were led to our cells, two or three of us in each one. The cells measured about six feet by ten feet; iron bunk beds with old and thin gray mattresses stood against the front bars on the right. To the rear and visible to anyone in the cell or walking by, were a toilet and a tiny sink. There were no windows in the cells, but up high on the other side of the corridor were small windows with views empty of everything but the color of the sky.

Freedom Riders, including me, were taken to
Parchman Prison's maximum security unit.

When we first arrived, I had to deal with Deputy Tyson, the head guard and the one who set the tone for all that was to come. He took away my asthma medication, accusing me of being a drug addict. Here it was, only the first day and I was already terrified. What would the coming struggle to breathe be like? I asked if I could see the prison doctor. "Sorry," Tyson announced, a nasty leer on his face, "the doctor is on vacation." I knew this to be false, as Parchman was a large prison farm with complete hospital facilities, but it was clear that arguing would get me nowhere except in more trouble.

It took two weeks before a doctor finally came. He talked to me through the bars and then declared that I was not a drug addict and could have my medication. With enormous relief, I saw Tyson come down the corridor with my inhaler in hand. But the respite didn't last long. When the doctor left a few minutes later Tyson came right back down the corridor, took the inhaler away, and I never saw it again.

We were allowed to leave our cramped quarters only twice a week for a shower in a small area at the end of the cell block. I longed for the forbidden opportunity to go outside in the open air, even if it was only to sit in a prison yard.

For part of the time I was at Parchman my cellmate was Peggy. She had short brown hair, a cheery smile, and was both easy and fun to be with. For exercise, we could walk up and down along the narrow space beside our bunk beds and the opposite wall. Others weren't so lucky—if there were three in the cell, the third mattress took up that space.

All reading material was prohibited except the Bible, which during my time there I succeeded in reading both testaments cover to cover. We could only get mail twice a week, though the guards often gave me hate mail rather than the letters from my family which I so anxiously awaited. The letters I received said things like: "God forbids integration of the races," and "Stop working for the Communists and start working for God." It was very common for people who approved of segregation to feel that anyone who protested against it was a communist.

Hot bright lights burned twenty-four hours a day. I could keep time only by the monotonous daily schedule: breakfast at six, lunch at noon, and dinner at five. For the most part the food was badly prepared grits and fatback that looked horrible and congealed on the plate. As there was no alternative, I had to force myself to get it down.

After the first week or so I began to have repetitive dreams. In the first, I was sitting on a swing, flying freely through the air, back and forth, back and forth, with my hair flowing out behind me in the warm breeze. The second was that I was feasting on lobster.

But despite these difficulties, prison life was not all bad. Although the individual cells were segregated, the cell block was not; and though we couldn't see each other except for those in our own cell, our voices were clear all along the corridor. We felt a deep connection to one another, all locked up for the same cause. Freedom songs rang out every day, filling the stale air with the soaring sound of the whole Civil

Rights Movement. "Oh Freedom," "Woke Up This Mornin' with My Mind Stayed on Freedom," "We Shall Overcome": all were songs derived from the spirituals sung in slave days. We sang and sang, nourishing ourselves and keeping our spirits up with the joy of our togetherness in this struggle. We ignored the guards' demands that we stop because we wanted them to know that, although they could imprison our bodies, our minds would remain free and strong. We felt victorious when we didn't give in to them. Many times they would punish us by coming through our block, clanking our doors open one by one and taking away our mattresses. When we continued to sing, they repeated their rounds and took our blankets, towels and toothbrushes. All that was left were our cold iron bed frames. Then they turned on the air conditioning full blast for hours, and yet we sang on with elation. Those nights we didn't get anything to eat, but we felt triumphant nevertheless.

We organized our days in a fairly loose manner. There was exercise period, when one of us would call out directions for walking back and forth in our cells, sit-ups, or anything else we might manage to do in such cramped quarters. There were times when we just talked, and times when we had quiet hour. It was during these silent times that I would go back to writing my prison diary on the few treasured pieces of paper given to me and which the jailers had let me keep.

Occasionally we had visits from church groups who prayed for us, hoping to lead us toward better ways. Their message, like the anonymous letters I received, usually called on us to turn away from Communist influences and bend back toward God.

The most memorable thing was our daily homemade "radio program." The same prisoner every day would shout out "Time for Parchman Hour." Then each cell, up and down the line, had to contribute something to entertain us and help pass the time: a song, a story, a joke—it didn't matter. That was when we had the privilege to hear true and glorious gospel singing soaring through the air into our cells and hearts. My cellmate Peggy and I had no such talents, but we did sing "like white people" and managed to do our part.

Peggy was brought up in an orphanage and was used to being treated badly. One day we saw Deputy Tyson standing in the corridor near us, the usual smirk on his callous face. He was staring at Cindy, the Freedom Rider in the cell next to ours. We later found out that he was watching her suffering a miscarriage, for which, as far as I know, she got no medical attention. Peggy said that that kind of sadism didn't really surprise her. For me, though, it was a cruelty that I could never have believed.

Time went by slowly. I actually wrote down the days of the month on a piece of paper and gladly crossed one off each evening. I came to realize how much life was taken from anyone in jail. I was only there for my thirty-nine days—what would it be like for years or even decades? For me, at least, there was meaning and purpose and deep friendship quickly reached, all of which were great compensation, but despite the solidarity and belief in what I was doing, I couldn't help wishing the day would come when I could walk out the door.

The Freedom Riders kept on coming and coming from all over the country, and by mid-September 1961 close to 400 of us had been jailed. The story was carried by newspapers and television throughout the country and woke people up to a situation that they might have known existed but hadn't paid much attention to.

Sadly, if it had only been African Americans who had been thrown in jail there would not have been all those stories publicizing arrests and brutal treatment. The suffering of black people never received much attention.

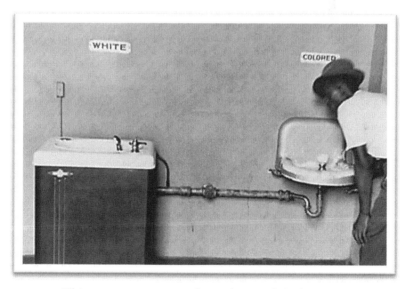

This was a common sight in the South before the Civil Rights Movement.

The never-ending news stories about our campaign finally led the Kennedy administration to enforce the existing but thus far never implemented federal law prohibiting segregation in all interstate facilities. Slowly, the hateful "white only" and "colored only" signs came down from the bus and train stations throughout the South, from their restaurants, their waiting rooms, their restrooms, and their water fountains.

What I'd read about in college, of a small and courageous integrated group taking a bus ride across the hostile South ended up not only achieving its own goal, but inspiring young people throughout the nation to participate in a Civil Rights Movement that grew beyond expectations in the years that followed. I learned that, even as one person, I could make a difference. Each individual can make a stand, and a crowd of them can change the world. None of us were aware of the part our actions would play in the long run; when you're present at the outset of historic change, it's never clear whether there will be any change at all. All we really had was intention, determination, hope, and each other.

The Freedom Rides offered me the opportunity to take part in the world as I had always dreamed of doing . . . to participate in something I believed in and set a path for me to follow for many years afterward.

FOUR
THE THIRTY-NINTH DAY

Ain't gonna' let nobody turn me 'round
Turn me 'round, turn me 'round
Ain't gonna' let nobody turn me 'round
I'm gonna' keep on a'walkin', keep on a'talkin'
Walkin' on to freedom land.

Verse from "Ain't Gonna Let Nobody Turn Me 'round."
Based on the spiritual "Let Nobody Turn You Around."

August 1961

Though the days at Parchman had only inched by as I marked them off on my wrinkled scrap of paper, the time to leave inevitably arrived. A trusty clanged open my cell door, gave me my street clothes and then left, saying he'd be back in half an hour. It was then that I quickly stuffed my diary in the hem of my gray and white striped seersucker skirt.

Soon the trusty came back to escort me—and the others whose time was up—down the hallway past the cells of the remaining Freedom Riders. As I passed each cell, I was torn between smiling and crying to show my love and support. I wanted to give every single woman a hug, but that wasn't possible as the trusty hurried us along through a large locked gate and down another somber corridor.

We picked up our few belongings at a small window and then went outside where a paddy wagon was waiting to take us to Jackson. There were big hugs all around, yet I found myself quite shaken. I was both elated to be free of my cell, but entirely lost as to where I was in my life.

My cellmate, Peggy. When would I ever see her again? All those women with whom I had shared so much. What would they do next? What would happen in their lives?

The interior of the paddy wagon was hot and stuffy with the summer heat of Mississippi as we retraced the road taken when I first came to Parchman. I remembered how curious I found the prison when I first arrived . . . the unnerving visible absence of people on the grounds, the buildings so windowless, non-descript and distant from each other. Now I knew I would never forget how far the South would go to prevent integration and the dehumanizing manner in which Parchman was operated. Later, as the Mississippi Delta country flowed by, conversations I'd had with my fellow prisoners flooded my mind. Peggy had told me a lot about her early life in the orphanage, how she had never felt special and loved, and how she had always identified with the underdog. Rose talked about her mother, who had registered to vote and had then lost her job. The financial stress that followed had led to family problems that ended in her Dad leaving, and an ongoing sadness in her heart.

The women in our cell block came from all over the country and had very different life stories, but the drama of our time together had bred a rare brand of closeness. I was sorry to walk away from the women who still had time to serve, even though I knew they would be OK. As time went by, thirty-nine days would pass for all of them. But together we had gone through something extraordinary. We had no idea of the place our individual and collective actions would play in history, yet each of us had risked doing what we thought was right and we had been together and united as we experienced the consequences.

Some years later the Congress of Racial Equality (CORE), the Student Nonviolent Coordinating Committee (SNCC), and the Southern Christian Leadership Conference (SCLC) would coordinate their anti-segregation efforts by forming the Congress of Federated Organizations (COFO), which established offices in many towns across the Deep South, bases where people working for civil rights could volunteer. But there was no such thing yet, so I was headed home.

When we eventually reached Jackson and had signed our bail agreements, there were many more hugs and some tears as we prepared to go our separate ways. Pulling myself away, I took the money that was still in my belongings and hailed a cab for the Jackson airport. An ache pressed against the inside of my ribs. For the first time in weeks I was without comrades, and I was scared and lonely.

When the cab arrived at the airport, I grabbed my tiny bag, headed for a shop where I bought a Gillette razor and then I went to the ladies room. I rubbed soapy water on my legs, and shaved them. There had been no mirror in my cell, but even in my idealistic state of mind I was obsessed with my fast growing leg hair: it was dark and, by then, long enough to catch anyone's eye. I hated it! I thought my legs looked like spider legs. Now the razor performed its magic, and once again I felt like a passable woman.

Fortunately I was able to get a flight leaving for Boston in a couple of hours. When I arrived at my gate and looked around, I realized again how noticeably different my appearance was from the well-dressed and stiffly coiffed women waiting to board, all of them white. I saw that they were looking at me, but I was free, and as unjust and inequitable as it was, I too, was white, making me feel both safe and angry.

How strange to be alone now in a world so different from where I had been since leaving Atlanta. Where was the punishing cruelty, where were the nasty words and insinuations? I knew my life had changed since I left home, but exactly how? The feeling of being let down after the weeks filled with so much purpose and close association left me almost stunned. How would what I had been through fit into my future? How would

I adjust to the much more ordinary existence I was about to re-enter? Would I be able to hold onto and act on my idealism, or would I slowly fall away into a life that would ultimately disappoint me?

Part Two

BETWEEN TWO WORLDS

FIVE
AUGUST 1961-SEPTEMBER 1964

It was a relief to finally arrive at home, and yet I hardly knew what to do with myself. I constantly felt a lump in my throat, and could barely believe that I was back in my childhood bedroom, awkward enough in itself, but even more so in light of all I had experienced and learned. The window beside my bed looked out on the same tree that had always been there as I grew up, which now seemed like eons ago. The walls were the same yellow color, the light wood dresser stood in the same place and the white, red and yellow print spreads still covered the twin beds. But it was almost impossible to recall the person I was when I lived there.

I couldn't relax. I kept feeling like I should be doing something more worthwhile, that time was being wasted, that I didn't know where to turn to make my days count. I was planning to go to graduate school in the fall, but wondered how I would fill in my life until then. All the questions that I had asked myself in the cab leaving Parchman still haunted me. Yes, it helped that my parents were so supportive, that my mother offered me steak three times a day to help cure the anemia caused by my time in prison, and that my brother Michael and my friends were available to hang out with. But still I was in a nowhere land between two worlds.

New people I met approached me only as a Freedom Rider, as if that defined me. I felt awkward and uncomfortable. "I'm just a regular person," I wanted to say. "There's nothing so special or different about me. Yes, going on a Freedom Ride is now part of me, but that's not all I am." It was difficult to establish new and real relationships.

A reporter from *The Boston Globe* interviewed me for the better part of two days. We sat facing each other on lawn chairs in my parents' back yard, and I was questioned endlessly for most of that time, with breaks for lunches and snacks. "Why did you do what you did?" she asked. "What experiences did you have during the ride and in prison? Were you afraid? How were you treated? What were your goals?" I answered all of those as best I could, as well as other questions I wish I had avoided, like "What did you wear? What did your parents think of what you did? What did they give you to eat in jail?"

When *The Boston Globe* printed the weeklong series, the first part of which was on the front page, I was embarrassed by the whole thing. There it was, a description of what I wore!

One of the headlines exclaimed, "My Diary Eluded the Jailers But My Mother Washed It Out." How humiliating for my poor Mom! Another lead was "Graduation Presents Spent to Buy Ticket for Trip to South." I was mortified that I had spilled out such unnecessary and trivial information during the long interview. Why would anyone think it was important enough to write in a newspaper about my clothing or finances? Where was the thoughtful discussion of the racial situation in the South or the aims of the Civil Rights Movement? Was it because I was a young woman that my story was trivialized this way?

But the articles were already out there in print. There was nothing I could do to change them.

Before long I was asked to talk to a church group about the Movement. I accepted, despite the anxiety I felt in front of crowds, because it was important to educate as many people as possible about the situation in Mississippi. I rehearsed over and over again, practically memorizing my whole presentation and consoling myself with the thought that nobody knew my experiences better than I. Driving to the church, I gripped the wheel tightly, still silently repeating the words I would say. When I walked up to the podium my brain seemed to freeze, but after I cleared my throat and forced out my first few words I discovered that I could speak and answer questions without embarrassing myself. I told the audience how I had come to the decision to go South and spoke about the goals of the Movement and how we planned to achieve them. I described some of the people I had been with, the rock solid racist attitudes we had to contend with, and what life was like for black people in the Deep South. I described prison life at Parchman.

And so followed a period when along with my regular life I spoke in churches, synagogues, and before civic groups, often enough so that I could jump in the car without planning anything, stand in front of a gathering, and speak naturally.

When fall arrived I started at Boston University's Graduate School of Education, headed toward a degree in speech therapy.

In the spring of 1963, while in my second year at Boston University, I turned on the television, and saw Bull Connor, still Commissioner of Public Safety in Birmingham, turn fire hoses and attack dogs on Civil Rights demonstrators. I watched in horror as the nonviolent protesters were mowed down and beaten, and wondered if any of my Parchman friends were among them. It felt strange and uncomfortable to be absent from the Movement. Was I letting myself and my friends down? Part of me wanted to finish school, while another part wanted to be back in Mississippi.

In 1963 I volunteered at the NAACP office on the corner of Massachusetts Avenue and Tremont Street in Boston. We were preparing for the March on Washington for Jobs and Freedom scheduled for August 28th. There was publicity to handle, people to sign up, and bus trips to organize. I loved being back in the midst of the Movement's goals and activities, and was happy to meet others in the Boston area such as Tom Atkins, a local black leader, and Reverend Jim

Breeden, a Freedom Rider, both of whom had also volunteered.

As midnight approached on the night before the March, buses from up and down the East Coast started to roll. I climbed onto one of the Boston buses and sat next to Betty, a volunteer with whom I had become friends. As I looked around I saw that every single seat was filled, and that, despite the time of day, everyone was totally energized. Even the air felt alive. The bus pulled out, and we were on our way, sometimes singing, sometimes chatting or eventually nodding off. It was a very long nine-hour trip, but we managed to arrive in Washington DC in time to walk toward the National Mall and find a place not very far from the Lincoln Memorial, where Martin Luther King Jr. would soon speak. I watched the broad empty space of the Mall behind me begin to fill the area surrounding the huge reflecting pool and beyond. The crowd, men and women of all colors and ages, swelled beyond anything I had ever seen or imagined. I could no longer see the end of the multitudes, and I was filled with exhilaration as I began to realize what a colossal event was occurring. Over the heads of 250,000 people rose thousands of protest signs demanding "First Class Citizenship Now," "Equal Rights Now," "Integrated Schools Now," and "We Demand an End to Police Brutality Now." Two-hundred and fifty thousand people might not sound like much nowadays, but for that time it was enormous.

The legendary gospel singer Mahalia Jackson opened the event with protest and church songs before we heard speeches by John Lewis, a leader of the Deep South protest movement (and a future United States Congressman) and A. Philip Randolph, president of the Brotherhood of Sleeping Car Porters. They were followed by almost deafening cheers as both Joan Baez and Bob Dylan stood up to sing protest songs.

And then, when Martin Luther King Jr. arrived at the podium, the crowd welcomed him with a joyous roaring and singing sound that must have been heard throughout the city. But an almost sacred hush fell upon the hundreds of thousands of people present when his sonorous voice rose and he began with "I am happy to join with you today in what will go down in history as the greatest demonstration for freedom in the history of our nation."

Martin Luther King talked about the huge suffering and heartbreak still caused by racism in this country, more than one hundred years after the Emancipation Proclamation. Though we were right to be elated by this huge event, he wanted us to never forget the pain, poverty, and humiliation that still existed and that had compelled us to come together.

I looked to the left and focused on the massive pillared memorial to Abraham Lincoln, author of the Emancipation Proclamation, and found myself fighting back tears. Next to me stood my friend Betty, and when I looked at her and others nearby, I discovered that I was not alone in my overflow of feeling. I felt incredibly lucky and privileged to be present, to be at this historic and overwhelming event.

Dr. King went on to encourage us to remain nonviolent: "Let us not satisfy our thirst for freedom by drinking from the cup of bitterness and hatred." He cautioned and heartened us: "We cannot walk alone." And: "We cannot turn back."

He filled us with resolve: "I am not unmindful that some of you have come here out of great trials and tribulations. And some of you have come from areas where your quest for freedom left you battered by the storms of persecution and staggered by the winds of police brutality. . . . [Let us] continue to work with the faith that unearned suffering is redemptive. Go back to Mississippi, go back to Alabama, go back to South Carolina, go back to Georgia, go back to Louisiana, go back to the slums and ghettos of our Northern cities, knowing that somehow this situation can and will be changed. . . . Let us not wallow in the valley of despair."

And then he went on to talk about his hopes and dreams for a future of freedom encompassing all races and religions; a future for his children and for all our future children, a future "when we will be able to all join hands and sing in the words of the old Negro spiritual: 'Free at last, free at last. Thank God Almighty we are free at last!'"

As I listened to these words, later to become known as Martin Luther King's "I Have a Dream" speech, my whole being was suffused with the truth and hope he spoke of. It was a magnificent prayer by a man whose life meant so much to his people, to this country, and to me.

The next month, as I was nearing the end of my time in graduate school, I went to visit my friend Betty. We sat on her living room couch watching the news and were horrified to learn of the four young girls, Carole Robertson, Addie Mae Collins, Cynthia Wesley and Carol Denise McNair, who were killed when a bomb placed by an angry white segregationist destroyed a black church in Birmingham, Alabama. Four such innocent young girls! Age-old racial hatred had struck again, and again my mind and heart turned to the Civil Rights Movement.

But despite my connection to the news from the South, I made a decision to stay in Massachusetts. I was close to graduation and wanted to finish my degree.

Early in 1964 my landlady in Cambridge, who had a reputation for dishonesty and cheating her tenants, turned off my heat and hot water for a couple of weeks, claiming that the boiler had broken down, something she did in all her buildings, one after another, like the wave at a Red Sox game. How would I get my dishes clean, and more importantly, how could I keep myself clean? Cold showers were not something that tempted me, and during the first week I went, towel in hand, to friends' apartments to take showers. At the beginning of the second week, needing another shower, I arrived unannounced to visit my brother Michael who lived with some friends in Allston. I knocked at the door, and someone I had never met before, a very tall and lanky guy named Sib, dressed in worn jeans and a blue denim shirt, answered. I said hello and excused myself to take my shower. Michael wasn't there, so when I finished, Sib and I sat in the living area and chatted. I liked him right away. He and I talked for a long time about all kinds of subjects and were excited and passionate about the same things. He was nothing like the men I'd recently dated. With them, I'd been so wary of drifting into the bland and uninvolved world they represented that I'm sure I unconsciously sabotaged practically every encounter. Among other things, Sib wanted to hear all about my time in the South. We talked for a while more, and I was smiling when I closed the door behind me.

The next week a snowstorm hit hard. The streets were slushy and icy, and there were snow drifts everywhere. My windows were iced up but my heat was back on and I was tucked in my cozy and warm little Cambridge apartment. There was a knock on the door, and it was Sib. He had walked all three miles from Allston. I whisked him in out of the cold wind and, pretending to be calm, asked if he would like something warm, perhaps some tea.

"Oh no," was the answer. "I just came to ask you if you want to see a play with me next week." I was so hoping that something like this would happen and was thrilled that he had come. Before even asking when the play was, I replied "I'd love to. But won't you stay for a while?"

"I really can't."

"Then why didn't you just call me?"

"I hate the phone." And then, after smiling and saying goodbye, he left.

Such a quirky guy. Another part of him that made me smile.

We began to spend a lot of time with each other. As much as I loved my parents, I always dreamed of living a life different from theirs, of finding someone who could be an exciting partner for me. So of course I was attracted to this man who cared so much about the world and was so easy to talk to, somewhat shy and so unexpectedly poetic.

The fact that we both loved adventure and wanted to do something useful in the world drew us even closer together. We decided to apply to the Peace Corps, but my application was denied because of my asthma. Eventually we talked about what would come next, and the following September we were married—and we headed almost immediately back to Mississippi.

Part Three
TROUBLE IN MERIDIAN, MISSISSIPPI

September 1964-August 1965

SIX
THE DANGERS OF TAXI RIDES

We shall live in peace, we shall live in peace
We shall live in peace someday
Oh deep in my heart, I do believe
We shall live in peace someday

Verse from "We Shall Overcome."
Based on a gospel song.

In October of 1964, Sib and I flew from Boston to Meridian, Mississippi. The June before, three young men working out of the Meridian COFO office—James Chaney, Andrew Goodman and Michael Schwerner—had been brutally murdered by the Ku Klux Klan, a secret and brutally violent white supremacist organization which has existed off and on since the late 1860's, and has used intimidation and murder to terrify African American people in order to keep them "in their place." In the past, in order to frighten their victims and retain their own anonymity, they often appeared in large groups wearing white pointed hats and sheets covering them from head to toe, only their eyes showing. At the time these three boys were killed, the Klan was quite prominent and was targeting activists in the Civil Rights Movement. Today, the Klan has lost most of its power, but still survives in small and scantly scattered groups.

After the murders of the three young men, we had been sent to help fill in the shocked and heartbroken gap left in the COFO staff. They needed more people to work on voter registration, the Freedom School that had been set up that summer, the picketing of segregated restaurants and hotels, and all the other efforts aimed at ending segregation and the ongoing brutality and humiliation targeting blacks.

When we entered the airport, I glanced around and, as in Jackson, was acutely aware of how conspicuous I was beside the Southern women with their conservative and well-groomed appearances. I had an attack of self-consciousness. Surely they were sizing me up, as I was them. My hair was always fighting any effort at control, and I was dressed in jeans and a cotton blouse. They must have seen me as unkempt and rebellious, and labeled me a hippie. They might even have guessed that I was a Civil Rights worker. I was very uncomfortable, and I'm sure Sib felt the same.

We went outside into the hot, humid air and hailed a cab. Taking a chance that the white driver wouldn't know the exact address of the COFO office, we asked the driver to take us to 25 5th Street. We rode through the unfamiliar outer city landscape with its low buildings and run down empty lots, and eventually pulled up beside a small and unobtrusive storefront on a busy street where all the pedestrians were black.

The COFO office Meridian Mississippi (1963).

We introduced ourselves to the workers in the tiny office crowded with furniture and supplies. They greeted us warmly, but were shocked that we had so naively put ourselves at the mercy of a white taxi driver.

"You two are crazy," was Greg's distressed response. "Don't you know the kind of things that go on here? That cab driver could have excused himself for a minute, made a quick call, and before you knew it, you'd be in the woods surrounded by the Klan! You drive a taxi when you can't do much of anything else; the drivers are poor and can be the types that end up in the Klan. How naïve can you be? You should have phoned us." By then he was pacing up and down with his head down and his hand on his forehead.

I thought to myself, "How stupid we are! I've been in Mississippi before. I know what it's like. How could we have let our guard down like that?" We stumbled through embarrassed apologies and vowed that we never again would hail a taxi in Mississippi.

But several months later we did do it once more, when we went to visit a local white family, cousins of a friend of ours in the North. It would be the first and only time that we'd be in the home of white Southerners. I wondered what the conversation would be like and especially how they would feel about what we were doing. I knew they were aware of our connection with COFO, but, after all, Meridian was their community, not ours. Would they feel, like most white Southerners, that we were "outside agitators" who had no business interfering with their way of life, no matter how illegal, brutal and pitiless it was? Were they inviting us only because our friend asked them to and they couldn't refuse?

Ralph and Amy lived on the outskirts of Meridian. (Although it was fifty years ago, I've followed Movement protocol and made up all the names that follow.) When I called Amy to make arrangements she advised us to walk to an inconspicuous downtown corner and take a cab to a shopping center not far from their house. Ralph would pick us up there. It was all very clandestine. There was no doubt that Amy was protecting her family by making sure there would be no way for anyone to identify us as Civil Rights workers if they happened to see us walking from Ralph's car to their front door.

When the time came, I put on a navy blue skirt, a white blouse and black sandals with low heels, my only shoes that could pass for slightly dressed up. I held my hair back in a large barrette. Sib and I followed Amy's directions, hailing a cab some distance from the COFO office and heading off to the shopping center. As soon as we got out of the cab, there was Ralph, welcoming us warmly. He had a million questions: "What are you working on? How long since you arrived? How is voting registration going?" What a relief! The ride was full of lively and easy talk. It was obvious that Ralph and Amy were going to be supportive.

We drove into a well-groomed neighborhood where paved sidewalks on both sides of the road were shaded by tall trees. Ralph turned into a driveway beside a split level house surrounded by meticulously cared-for gardens, and pulled around to the back.

As we entered their house, we were greeted by Amy and their two young daughters, Joanie (age seven), and Linda (age ten). They were both dressed in pressed cotton pants and t-shirts that looked brand new. Their hair was neatly combed.

We were invited into the living room where we sat on a pale green couch across from large windows looking out on the gardens. The girls went upstairs, Amy brought in drinks, and talk began.

Amy's first sentence surprised us. She asked us if we would please not talk about what we were doing in Mississippi in front of Joanie and Linda. She and Ralph glanced at each other and then took turns explaining their situation to us. "You see," Ralph said, "we're both glad you're here. We both hate what's going on in the South. It's not the way we were brought up back home and it's not the way we'd like to live. The changes you're working for are changes we support."

"But," Amy continued almost pleadingly, her eyes fastening on us, "we have to protect Joanie and Linda. We can't tell them how we feel about race relations here. They're too young to understand that if they repeat our views in school, especially to the older children, they would certainly be ostracized and could even get beaten up. I hate not being able to teach them what's right." And then, closing her eyes, she added, "But I can't bear to think of them being hurt."

What was there to say? What I thought was, "Why do you live here, feeling as you do? Why don't you move? Isn't it more important to live by your conscience?" But my heart went out to them. I didn't have a family to support. I didn't have a business that couldn't easily be moved elsewhere. I didn't have two little girls whom I loved more than anything in the world and needed to keep from harm. I certainly wasn't in their shoes. I felt frustrated and angry at the situation. If only Amy and Ralph could walk picket lines with us and perhaps, just perhaps, inspire some of their friends to join in.

We had dinner with the girls, and after they got bored with us and left again to go play, we continued our conversation. Ralph had a factory in Meridian which enabled him to make a decent living. He was also a partner in the black movie theatre around the corner from our office. "So here's how it works," he explained. "There's a much nicer movie theatre downtown for white people. Black people can go there but can only sit in the balcony. In my theatre, usually only black people come. But every so often there's a movie which would never be shown in the white theatre but which we would like to see, as would some of our more open-minded friends. So what do we do? We go to my theatre, wait outside until the lights go down, and then we sneak up to the balcony. That's how we saw *A Raisin in the Sun*, that's how we saw *The Defiant Ones*, and *Nothing but a Man*. We sneak out just as the movie is ending. Any other way of doing it, the word would surely get out."

Ralph looked at us with a painful smile on his face. "Isn't this just crazy," he sighed. "How can a system be so vicious and so ludicrous at the same time?"

We finished our dessert and said our fond goodbyes to Ralph, Amy, and the girls. Ralph drove us back to the shopping center where we again hailed and boarded a cab.

When we arrived home, Sib and I talked about how sad the visit was. Neither one of us felt that we could live the way

Ralph and Amy did. Though black people in Mississippi were living with enormous fear and anger, it was clear that some white people had their own version of dread to deal with, enough so that it kept them silent in the face of a system they abhorred.

SEVEN

FANNIE LEE CHANEY:

A Mother's Loss

We've been 'buked and we've been scorned
We've been talked about sure's you're born
But we'll never turn back.
No we'll never turn back
Until all the people are free
And we have equality

A verse from "We'll Never Turn Back."

It was a cool evening in early December when I walked along with Sib and a few other Civil Rights workers, making our way from the COFO office in Meridian to Fannie Lee Chaney's house. James Chaney, Fannie Lee's twenty-one-year-old son, was one of the three Civil Rights workers killed by the Ku Klux Klan earlier that year.

Fannie Lee Chaney and son Ben at James Chaney's funeral. James Chaney, Andrew Goodman, and Michael Schwerner were abducted and murdered by the Klan in Neshoba County, Mississippi in June 1964 during the Civil Rights Movement.

In the South of those days, small black and white neighborhoods of no more than a very few blocks were interspersed with each other in checkerboard fashion. Though I had been in Mississippi for several months, this peculiarity, so unlike the district-wide mostly segregated neighborhoods of the North, still caught my attention. First we would walk by a series of freshly painted houses surrounded by groomed lawns, each one with a paved driveway sporting a pick-up truck or shiny car. We could see backyard jungle gyms and wading pools through the spaces between each house. Here and there a hired black man doggedly pushed a lawnmower. Then suddenly, for a few blocks, we would be in a black neighborhood: faded, rundown homes with peeling paint and sagging porches, an occasional old vehicle on a dirt track, and more dirt than grass on their postage stamp-sized front yards.

All the time my eyes darted from side to side, aware that a police car might appear and roll slowly past us, or worse yet, some white thugs in a pick-up truck, howling with hate at the integrated future we represented. I was on high alert, as if walking in a strange and perilous jungle hearing growls in the underbrush.

When we arrived at Fannie Lee's house, the rich aroma of her cooking greeted us. Fannie Lee had a lovely round face, high cheekbones, and a soft welcoming manner. That night her dark skin was a bit shiny in the heat from her stove. She wore a loose dress with a faded pattern of blue and yellow flowers, and on top of that a grayish apron with a torn pocket and frayed edges.

Her kitchen was small and immaculate, but poorly lit. An old white enamel stove stood against a faded green wall. Some of us sat at her simple rectangular wooden table set along a wall perpendicular to the stove. Others stood talking to Fannie Lee, or just milling around. Fannie Lee's two surviving children were also there: Ben (age twelve), who loved to hang out at the COFO office with us, and his older sister Barbara, who loved to tease us by dividing the races into two groups which she labeled "colored" and "colorless."

Although the dark feeling of danger still pressed around us, right then I was able to close Fannie Lee's door on it. I felt enveloped by her generous and brave spirit and by the common goal we all shared. In the crowded kitchen everyone was busy talking and eating. We never lacked subjects to discuss: Sib being thrown in a one-room county jail with a dirt floor for an allegedly broken taillight (it wasn't broken); Sandy Watts spending weeks in the Meridian jail for unwittingly receiving a stolen radio that had been donated to our office; or the picket line that we were planning for the following week.

Later in the evening, after Fannie Lee's delicious dinner, the conversation slowed and I heard Fannie Lee say, "Ah, it's all my fault. I never should have let him leave the house that day." As if she could have known. "If it was only my son James," she continued, "the courts would be ignoring it, but he was killed with those two white boys, so now they'll *have* to do something."

James was a local Civil Rights activist who had joined forces with Michael Schwerner and Andrew Goodman, both of whom had come to Mississippi for the 1964 Freedom Summer. On June 21st, just a few months before our dinner with Fannie Lee, the three of them had gone to the small rural town of Philadelphia in Neshoba County to check out the firebombing of the Mount Zion Methodist Church, which had been used for voter registration rallies. On their way back to Meridian, the boys were arrested by Neshoba County Sheriff's Deputy Cecil Price, who brought them to the town jail in Philadelphia, Mississippi.

Andrew Goodman, James Chaney, and Michael Schwerner pictured on an FBI Missing poster displayed in 1964.

Later that night they were released, but only after Cecil Price had secretly informed Ku Klux Klan members of their route back to Meridian. It was forty-four days before their bodies were finally discovered buried in an earthen dam. According to the FBI investigation report, James's body was a "mangled mass." Unlike the other two men, he had been brutally tortured before he was shot.

Our hearts were heavy in the silence following Fannie Lee's outpouring. I was overwhelmed with my inability to find a word worthy of saying in the face of such tragedy, anger, and grief. People got up to hug Fanny Lee and offer softly spoken words of comfort, and I joined them. Ben and Barbara were right next to her, Ben holding her hand. Then, after some subdued conversation, there were more hugs all around, and some murmured goodbyes as we filed back out into the street.

The next time I saw Fannie Lee was on a drizzling day three weeks later, on December 10th, 1964. Nineteen Klan members, including Deputy Sheriff Cecil Price and Neshoba County Sheriff Lawrence Rainey, had been arrested by the FBI. A preliminary hearing was being held at the federal courthouse in Meridian to decide whether the cases of these men should be sent to the Grand Jury. Since only states can bring charges of murder, and Mississippi refused to do so, the U.S. Attorney's office had taken over, but could only bring the outrageously feeble charge of violating the three young men's civil rights.

About one hundred people were allowed into the wood-paneled courtroom, while at least that many more could not be accommodated. Some of them crowded together outside the door with their faces pressed against the glass panels. I sat with twenty or so local black people and COFO workers on a long bench about halfway back. I wasn't actually expecting anything legal and fair to be decided, but I still clung to some little bit of hope. The guilt of these men seemed so clear that maybe, just this once, justice might prevail. Maybe this time, all the recent publicity would force some kind of appropriate outcome. Maybe, finally, the murder of a black person or a white sympathizer would be deemed a crime rather than service to the community.

Sheriff Rainey (right) and Deputy Sheriff Price at arraignment hearing in 1964 in Meridian, Mississippi.

The defendants were arranged in rows behind a wooden railing to the front of us and to the left. A sick feeling went through me when I saw Sheriff Rainey with his heavy-booted foot slung up on his other knee, showing his hairy calf. He was slouched down, his big belly creating a mound under his tight shirt. He held an enormous bag of Red Man Tobacco, and his cheeks bulged out like balloons ready to pop. He was clearly the leader, clowning with his followers, and his mouth was open in a huge repulsive grin. Next to him was Deputy Sheriff Price with a confident smirk on his face. Others sitting back further included Alton Wayne Roberts, brother of Lee Roberts, a local white Meridian policeman who was well known for the endless illegal ways he found to harass us, including almost daily trumped up driving violations.

All the defendants grinned and whispered to each other, every single one cocksure that the great state of Mississippi would never, not ever, prosecute them for getting rid of who these men referred to as "that n—— and the two white agitators."

Was this a scene out of a movie? I had seen things like this portrayed on film, but always thought they were exaggerated. The overweight, cocky white lawman in the movie who knew that his every bigoted and hateful move against black people would be supported and applauded by the majority of the white community. The policeman's shiny boot on the neck of a prone black man was still being cheered and was not about to be lifted.

The hearing began. The evidence for the prosecution consisted of a signed confession by one of the defendants, Horace Doyle Barnette. Commissioner Esther Carter, in charge of the hearing, refused to admit the signed statement because, she insisted, only one FBI agent had heard it and, since Barnette was not in the courtroom, it had to be considered only hearsay evidence. Enraged, the prosecuting attorney jumped to his feet. But Carter was adamant, and the small hope that I sheltered began to sputter and disappear, like a small fire extinguished for lack of air.

In the end, all the accused were released without having to post bail. Esther Carter had dismissed the charges.

My shoulders slumped and I groaned softly, my head in my hands. I looked down the bench at my co-workers and saw similar poses and some tears. I heard cheering from various white people in the courtroom, but it was the sounds of anguish that overwhelmed all else.

As we left the courthouse, the defendants and their lawyers were slapping each other on the back, laughing and congratulating each other. Outside the building, an old black woman was kneeling on the sidewalk crying, "Jesus, No! Jesus, No!"

Nearby, Fannie Lee stood in her gray coat with her head bent. I could see only her back but she was holding onto Barbara and Ben, and her shoulders were heaving.

◊

In 1967 the Klansmen who murdered Andrew Goodman, James Chaney, and Michael Schwerner were finally tried. Seven of them were found guilty, nine were acquitted (including Sheriff Rainey), and the jury was unable to reach a decision on three others. After unsuccessful appeals, the seven went to prison.

Price served three years.

◊

The following is a transcript of the speech that Fannie Lee Chaney delivered at the ruins of the Mt. Zion Church in

Neshoba County on the day of the memorial service for James Chaney, Michael Schwerner, and Andrew Goodman. The transcript of this speech comes from a letter written by Luke Kabat, one of the Civil Rights workers in Meridian.

Well, you all know that I am Mrs. Chaney, the mother of James Chaney. You all know what my child has done. He was trying so hard and he had two fellows from New York, owned their own house and everything—didn't have nothin' to worry about. They came here to help us. Did you all know they came here to help us? They died for us. They died for us. Now, is we gonna let this be in vain? I can't let my child's work go in vain. And his two companions. That boy, Mickey Schwerner— he was just like a son of mine. He was just like my son. James was my son. James told me when he came from Canton, he said "Mamma, you just don't know—there's a heap here yet that you don't know." I say, "Whatchu mean?" He say, "Mamma, you just don't half know. I went to school two weeks in Jackson, and Mamma, I learnt somethin'. I learned more than I learned in 9 months at Harris High and all the 16 years I went to school. And I learned somethin' in them two weeks." That's what my child said. He was just as well, and I was glad of it. And I was layin' across the bed. He said, "You know what, Mamma?" And I said "What?" He said "Micky, I never known a man on earth who could live like him." I said "Whatchu mean?" He said "Mamma, that man got sense. I'll go with him and I'll die for him. And I'll do anything he tell me to do." He say, "Because, Mamma, he came here to help us and I'm not going to let him do it by hisself." He say, "I'm going with him and I'll be with him." I say "Son, well, if that's what you want, I'm with you. I'm with you and Mickey both." And that was my child. And Mickey and Andrew—they was mine too. And I don't want these children's work to be lost—I don't want those children's work to be lost. They gone. They was beaten, they was dogged. Now we gonna let all of that die? We gonna let that die? No! We can't let that die. No sir, I'll never let my child's life go in vain. I wanna know if somebody's gonna help me. (The crowd answers 'yes'.) I say you all gonna help me. I said I was gonna say nothing, but I couldn't stand up here, sit up here. I gotta say somethin. My child go nights out here to this church. Set up the first mass meeting. Right here. Next time he came back here it was burned down. Who was it who burned this church so. For why?

Now it's time for we to pray. It's time for us to be close now. And if we gonna do somethin', we better try to do it now. I want help. I want help. And I need all of you all.

Everybody up yonder, they helpin' us. They was behind me 100%. Everywhere I went. Behind me 100%. But right here at home, that's where I need help. And I'm lookin' for you all to help me. Don't let those children's work go in vain. They dead. Don't let their work die. That's when freedom started. When they beat, destroyed, and 'buked (rebuked) my child and those other boys. That's when freedom started. You all don't know. You all got parents, and they got lots of children that's gone. But none of them went like mine. It's hard. It's hard. But every time there is somethin' about freedom, I go. I got to go. When my children come home this evening, my head was hurtin'. They say, "Mamma, you goin'?" I say "Yes, I'm goin'. I'm sure goin'", even if nobody else don't go. I'm goin". And here I am.

◊

The following is the signed statement which was furnished to the FBI by Horace Doyle Barnett on November 19, 1964.

I, Horace Doyle Barnette, do hereby make this free and voluntary statement to SA Henry Rask and SA James A. Wooten, who have identified themselves to me to be special agents of the Federal Bureau of Investigation and SA Henry Rask have informed me that I do not have to make a statement, that any statement made by me can be used against me in a court of law and that I am entitled to consult with an attorney before making this statement and that if I can not afford an attorney and I am required to appear in court, the court will appoint one for me. That no force, threats or promises were made to induce me to make this statement.

I presently reside at Cullen, La. I am 26 years old and was born on September 11, 1938, at Plaindealing, La.

On June 21, 1964 about 8:00 P.M., I was having supper at Jimmy Arledge's house, Meridian, Mississippi. Travis Barnette called Arledge on the telephone and told Arledge that the Klan had a job and wanted to know if Arledge and I could go. Arledge asked me if I could go and we went to Akins trailer park on Highway 80 in Meridian, Miss. We did not know what this job was.

Upon arriving at Akins Trailer Park we were met by Preacher Killin, Mr. Akins, Jim Jordan, and Wayne. I do not know Wayne's last name, but I do know his brother is a police officer in Meridian, Miss. Killin told us that three civil rights workers were in jail in Philadelphia, Miss., and that these three civil rights workers were going to be released from jail and that we were going to catch them and give them a whipping. We were given brown cloth gloves and my car was filled with gas from Mr. Akins' gas tank. Jim Snowden, who works for Troy Laundry in Meridian came to Akins Trailer Park too.

Arledge, Snowden, and Jordan got into my car and we drove to Philadelphia. Killin and Wayne left before we did and we were told that we should meet him there. Killin had a 1962 or 1961 white Buick.

When we arrived in Philadelphia, about 9:30 P.M. we met Killin and he got into my car and directed me where to park and wait for someone to tell us when the three civil rights workers were being released from jail.

While we were talking, Killin stated that 'we have a place to bury them, and a man to run the dozer to cover them up.' This was the first time I realized that the three civil rights workers were to be killed.

About 5 or 10 minutes after we parked a patrolman from Philadelphia came to the car and said that 'they are going toward Meridian on Highway 19. We proceeded out Highway 19 and caught up to a Mississippi State Patrol car, who pulled into a store on the left hand side of the road. We pulled along side of the patrol car and then another car from Philadelphia pulled in between us. I was driving a 1957 Ford, 4 door, 2 tone blue bearing Louisiana license. The Philadelphia car was a 1958 Chevrolet 2 door and color maroon. It also had a dent on front right hand fender next to the light. No one got out of the cars, but the driver of the Philadelphia car, who I later learned was named Posey, talked to the patrolmen. Posey then drove away and we followed.

About 2 or 3 miles down the highway Posey's car stopped and pulled off on the right hand side of the road. Posey motioned for me to go ahead. I then drove fast and caught up to the car that the three civil rights workers were in, pulled over to the side of the road and stopped. About a minute or two later, Deputy Sheriff Price came along and stopped on the pavement beside my car. Jordan asked him who was going to stop them and Price said that he would and took after them and we followed. The Civil Rights workers turned off Highway 19 on to a side road and drove about a couple of miles before Price stopped them. Price stopped his car behind the 1963 Ford Fairlane Station Wagon driven by the Civil Rights Workers and we stopped behind

Price's car. Price was driving a 1956 Chevrolet, 2 door and 2 tone blue in color.

Price stated 'I thought you were going back to Meridian if we let you out of jail.' The Civil Rights Workers stated that they were and Price asked them why they were taking the long way around. Price told them to get out and get into his car. They got out of their car and proceed[ed] to get into Price's car and then Price took his blackjack and struck Chaney on the back of the head.

At the junction of Highway 19 and where we turned off, I had let Arledge out of the car to signal the fellows in the Philadelphia car. We then turned around and proceeded back toward Philadelphia. The first car to start back was Price and he had Jim Jordan in the front seat with him and the three civil rights worker[s] in the back seat. I followed next and picked up Arledge at the junction of Highway 19. Snowden drove the 1963 Ford, belonging to the Civil Rights Workers.

When we came to Posey's car Price and Snowden pulled over to the left side of the Highway and stopped in front of Posey's car. I stopped behind it. Wayne and Posey and the other men from Philadelphia got into the 1963 Ford and rode with Snowden. I do not know how many men were from Philadelphia. Price then started first and I pulled in behind him and Snowden driving the 1963 Ford came last.

I followed Price down Highway 19 and he turned left on to a gravel road. About a mile up the road he stopped and Snowden and I stopped behind him, with about a car length between each car. Before I could get out of the car Wayne ran past my car to Price's car, opened the left rear door, pulled Schwerner out of the car, spun him around so that Schwerner was standing on the left side of the road with his back to the ditch and said 'Are you that n—— lover?' and Schwerner said 'Sir, I know just how you feel'. Wayne had a pistol in his right hand, then shot Schwerner.

Wayne then went back to Price's car and got Goodman, took him to the left side of the road with Goodman facing the road, and shot Goodman.

When Wayne shot Schwerner, Wayne had his hand on Schwerner's shoulder. When Wayne shot Goodman, Wayne was standing within reach of him.

Schwerner fell to the left so that he was laying alongside the road. Goodman spun around and fell back toward the bank in back.

At this time Jim Jordan said 'save one for me.' He then got out of Price's car and got Chaney out. I remember Chaney backing up, facing the road, and standing on the bank on the other side of the ditch and Jordan stood in the middle of the road and shot him. I do not remember how many times Jordan shot. Jordan then said, 'You didn't leave me anything but a n——, but at least I killed me a n—— .''

The three civil rights workers were then put into the back of their 1963 Ford wagon. I do not know who put the bodies in the car, but I only put Chaney's foot inside the car.

Price then got into his car and drove back toward Highway 19. Wayne, Posey and Jordan then got into the 1963 Ford and started up the road. Snowden, Arledge and another person who I do not know the name of got into my car and we followed. I do not know the roads we took, but went through the outskirts of Philadelphia and to the Dam site on Burrage's property.

When we arrived at the Dam site someone said that the bulldozer operator was not there and Wayne, Arledge and I went in my car to find him. We drove out to a paved road and about a mile down the road we saw a 1957

Chevrolet, white and green, parked on the left side of the road. Wayne told me to stop and we backed up to this car. Burrage and 2 other men were in the car. Wayne said that they were already down there and Burrage said to follow them. I followed the 1957 Chevrolet back toward the Dam site, taking a different road, until the Chevrolet stopped. Burrage said 'It's just a little ways over there,' and Wayne and the bulldozer operator walked the rest of the way. The bulldozer operator was about 40 years old, 6 ft 2 inches tall, slim built and a white male. He was wearing khaki clothes. Arledge and I then followed Burrage and the other man back to Burrage's garage. The other man was a white male, about 40 years old, 5 feet 8 or 9 inches tall, stocky built. Burrage's garage is on the road toward Philadelphia and he had tractors and trailer[s] parked there. His house is across the road.

We were there about 30 minutes when the other fellows came from the dam site in the 1963 Ford. Burrage got a glass gallon jug and filled it with gasoline to be used to burn the 1963 Ford car owned by the three civil rights workers. Burrage took one of the diesel (sic) trucks from under a trailer and said 'I will use this to pick you up, no one will suspect a truck on the road this time at night.' It was then about 1:00 to 1:30 in the morning.

Snowden, Arledge, Jordan, Wayne and I then got into my car and we drove back toward Philadelphia. When we got to Philadelphia a city patrol car stopped us and we got out. Sheriff Rainey, Deputy Sheriff Price and the City Patrolman, who told us which way the civil rights workers were leaving town, got out of the patrol car. The patrolman was a white male about 30 years old, 5 feet 8 to 9 inches, 160 lbs, and was wearing a uniform. This was about 2:00 AM., June 22, 1964. I do not know his name, but I have met him before and would know him again.

We talked for 2 or 3 minutes and then someone said that we better not talk about this and Sheriff Rainey said 'I'll kill anyone who talks, even if it was my own brother.'

We then got back into my car and drove back to Meridian and passed Posey's car which was still parked along side the road. We did not stop and there was one or two men standing by Posey's car. We then kept going to Meridian. I took Wayne home, left Jordan and Snowden at Akins Mobile Homes, took Arledge home and went home myself.

I have read the above statement, consisting of this and 9 other pages and they are true and correct to the best of my knowledge and belief. I have signed my initials to the bottom of the first 9 pages and initial[ed] mistakes. No force, threats or promises were made to induce me to make this statement.

/s/
Horace Doyle Barnette

EIGHT
LUKE'S STRUGGLE FOR CIVIL RIGHTS

Stand up and rejoice, a great day is here
We are fighting Jim Crow and the victory is near
Hallelujah I'm a travelin', hallelujah ain't it fine?
Hallelujah I'm a travelin', down freedom's main line.

Verse from "Hallelujah I'm a Travelin'"
by Chris Vallillo.

Most days in Meridian, I'd be planning a demonstration or checking out finances at my desk in the COFO office at about three o'clock when school got out. It wouldn't be long before my little ten-year-old friend Patty Thompson would come flouncing in the door, usually followed closely by Lenray and Lance, all three of their faces lightened by enormous toothy smiles. Welcoming the fun and liveliness they brought with them, I grinned right back.

Luke Kabat surrounded by local school kids outside the COFO office in Meridian, Mississippi.

They loved being in our space and were almost daily visitors, partly because of the activities there, and partly because it was a real novelty for them, as black children, to hang around with an integrated group including white people who actually encouraged and enjoyed their company. I was especially close to Patty and always looked forward to her visits. Somehow our hearts had just bonded. She would sit beside me and we'd talk about all the little things in her life. Sometimes she would want to feel my hair... then I would feel hers.

The three kids pranced around the long thin room, wanting attention from each and every one of us. But it was really only a polite delay before what they really were after came right out. "Where's Luke? Is he here? Is he here?"

"He'll be back in a few minutes," Sam, a local high school volunteer, answered. "There's some paper and pens over on that table. You kids can go over there and draw while you're waiting for him."

The COFO office was also a huge draw for teenagers beginning to feel their power to take part in social change. It was here that they could find each other and, in spite of the risk, participate in whatever protest activities were going on. Betty Manuel, fifteen or so, had shaved her head. As she explained to Luke in Freedom School, "The reason for deciding to shave my head and let my hair grow in natural was that I feel that straightening of hair is a sign of the Negro being ashamed of being a Negro and wants to be more like the white man. It shows that the Negro thinks the white man's standard of beauty is the only way to judge beauty. I want to show people that I am not ashamed of my hair texture."

This was quite a statement for Betty, who was just a teenager at the time. The standards of beauty then were based on white peoples' features and most black women straightened their hair. Betty was at a time in her life when, for most people, "How do I look today?" was a huge issue. Yet she had the courage to put herself out there in front of all her friends and schoolmates to stand up for what she believed.

The younger ones who hung around our office came mainly because they just loved the atmosphere. But all of them, high school age down to six or seven, had a special place in their hearts for Luke, as he did for each of them.

When the COFO door swung open and Luke Kabat, dressed in his usual dark jeans and plaid shirt, would arrive, all attention would turn toward him. He was slim, with dark hair, and appealing New York Jewish looks. At once Lenray, Patty, and Lance would drop what they were doing and rush over to him, trying to get hold of whatever part of his body they could capture . . . a hand, a shoulder, even a finger. Then they would all be enclosed and wrapped in his affection. None were left out.

And these young people weren't the only ones drawn to Luke. Each one of us had a special feeling for him. His compassion enveloped not only the victims of racism, but all those in the world who were left out, who couldn't reach their potential for whatever reason. There wasn't one of us who didn't feel at home with him, who didn't trust him, who didn't feel his love and respect.

Luke taught Freedom School, often with Gail Falk. COFO had space in an old building in Meridian where kids in the area would show up after regular school hours to learn about black history and to discuss present-day issues. About 150 kids took part, despite the fact that the older ones were threatened with expulsion from Harris High, the segregated high school for black students. In addition to black history, Freedom School classes included biology, history, algebra, art, and English. In a biology class Luke once dissected a dead field mouse that the kids had found. He also showed them human skin under a microscope, making sure they understood that skin color was just that, no more than skin deep.

Inspired by Martin Luther King Jr.'s "I Have a Dream" speech in August of 1963, Luke and Gail had the kids write their own "I Have a Dream" ideas, to talk about their own hopes for the future, both personal and concerning race relations.

Willie Clark dreamed that "someday people will be as lovely as the world." Artie dreamed that "one day I can walk down the street knowing that I can stop in any place if I get hungry." Delores dreamed about "joining the Air Force, going to Paris, getting married, and sending for my mother and brother and father." Barbara Chaney, sister of the murdered Civil Rights worker James Chaney, dreamed "that Sheriff Rainey would be electrocuted."

Luke wrote about his dream for all the wallflowers of the world... h e envisioned that they would be able to leave their safe hiding places, come into the light, and join the dance.

Although I was in Meridian because I wanted to fight segregation and all the vicious and frightening behavior that went along with it, I'm not sure that most of us white workers really understood all the intricate and complicated shades of rage, shame, fear, and especially courage, experienced by those who had suffered racial tyranny for generations. But I believe that Luke innately grasped the whole picture. He got it all: the depth of anger and hatred, the terror, the heartbreak, and the everyday humiliation of being seen as inferior. He could talk about these things.

He was also a medical student. What a doctor he would have made! When I think of him I think of the gentle and happy feeling we all had when near him. I think of not just his anger, but his deep sadness in the face of what we were fighting. And I think of his joy in life and his unassuming smile.

During his time in Meridian, Luke wrote a letter about the memorial service for James Chaney that took place about a week after the bodies of Chaney, Schwerner, and Goodman were discovered. (See Chapter Seven, "Fannie Lee Chaney: A Mother's Loss.") He said that he and Gail Falk felt there should be a march before the funeral, a slow walk by local citizens that would not only speak of everyone's heartache and anger, but give local people an opportunity to be with each other at a time of such anguish and tragedy.

To protect the march from Klan interference, the day of the service was announced only the evening before. Luke and Gail stayed up all night printing thousands of fliers announcing that there would be three gathering places, three churches in different parts of town, and that groups would walk from there to the First Union Baptist Church where the funeral would take place.

Luke (center, in dark suit) at the Mount Zion Methodist Church in Neshoba County during the memorial service for James Chaney, Andrew Goodman, and Michael Schwerner. This memorial service took place a while after the funeral for James Chaney in Meridian, and it is where Fannie Lee Chaney gave her speech to hundreds of people.

The next afternoon people began to leave their homes and head toward the churches. Small groups in dark clothing gathered in silence at street corners and joined other groups coming from other directions. Old men and women limped along as best they could, their tired feet following the still hoped for road to Freedom. Luke walked along and yelled out to whoever might hear, "Come and join us. We're going to James Chaney's funeral. He died for us. Help us carry on his work." What started out as individuals, each one determined to publicly stand up and refuse to give into fear, became a powerful stream leaving each church and then a mighty river as everyone joined together to remember what James Chaney had done and to continue his struggle. As Luke said in his letter, "We all died a little with him. Now we must live a little for him."

The next year, after most of us had left Mississippi, after Sib had started law school in Boston, and after Luke had met and married a lovely woman named Syrtiller, we were wakened one night by the phone ringing. It was Luke calling from California to tell us that he had lung cancer. He had gone to a wedding and was shocked to realize that he couldn't walk across the parking lot without struggling for breath. It turned out that the cancer was already all over his body.

Not Luke! Not that beautiful man! I felt the wrenching loss of something so precious in this world, someone so unique and so loved by us. Neither Sib nor I could find the right words on the phone that night. Nothing was adequate.

I wanted to call Luke back the next day. Sib wanted to write him a loving and hopeful letter. But we couldn't imagine what to say, how to comfort him in any way. So, though thinking about it constantly, we put it off. It was our first experience with cancer and how fast it can travel.

We waited too long. Luke died very soon after his call to us. When we heard the news, we sat in our living room with Gail Falk, aching at his loss and horrified that we never responded to his tragic phone call. Why hadn't we rushed off to California to be with him? Why hadn't we called every day? Why hadn't we realized how fast this could happen?

We lost our chance.

Later we would name our wonderful son after Luke. How I wish Luke Kabat could have met him . . . he would have been so proud of his namesake. The first Luke's mother came to see us, to meet our son, and to bring him a beautiful, colorful Mexican candelabra filled with hanging birds, flowers and sweet painted animals. As I look at it now in our son's home, I am each time still aware of the gentle waterfall of loving feelings that fill me up. It's now, shockingly, more than fifty years since Luke died. How glad I am that we knew him. How sad I am at the empty space he left behind.

NINE

LIVING WITH THE LANIERS

Go tell it on the mountain
Over the hills and everywhere
Go tell it on the mountain
To let my people go.

Verse from "Go Tell it on the Mountain."
Based on a traditional Christmas song about the birth of
Christ.

What did it take for Mississippi black families to risk everything by hosting white Civil Rights workers from the north? For Sib and me, it was Robert Lanier and his wife, Johnnie Ruth, who had the courage to share their home with us. The most likely danger for them, if the wrong people found out, was that Robert would lose his job and have trouble finding another one, at least among white employers. Beyond that, in those years, who could say what might occur.

Johnnie Ruth stayed home, kept house, did the shopping and tended to their infant son, who was called "Flap." I can't remember what Robert did for work, but I know that every day he came home exhausted. He also had a divinity school education, so that he was often addressed as Reverend Lanier and was frequently out in the evenings and on weekends, committed to pastoral duties.

The Lanier's house was in a well-tended black neighborhood and quite small. They had the front bedroom, the back one was ours. Like other families who took in Civil Rights volunteers, Robert and Johnnie Ruth were devoted to the Movement and did whatever they could to be of service. It was an every day commitment, sometimes for many months. Along with the dangers they might face, they had to deal with two additional adults in the house, the extra food needed and the lack of privacy. The Laniers did so with generosity and welcoming arms, never making us feel like we were imposing.

Sometimes I would hang out with Johnnie Ruth and play with Flap. The three of us went on walks in the neighborhood together and I often sat on the floor with Flap and his toys. When I showed Flap how to blow into a harmonica, he was first startled and then full of glee.

The Laniers asked Sib and me if we would like to go to church with them on Sunday mornings. Wanting to take part in as much of their culture as possible, we gladly agreed. Warm welcomes greeted us when we first arrived at the modest building, and every Sunday thereafter. We sang hymns with the parishioners and truly enjoyed being able to participate.

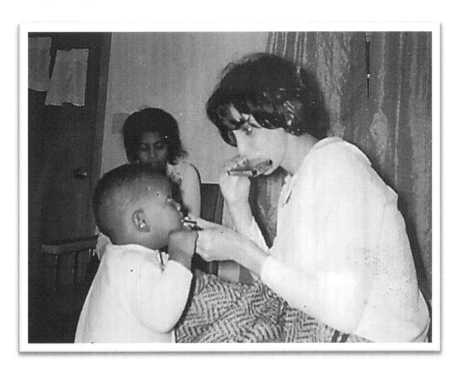

Johnnie Ruth watches while I
show "Flap" Lanier how to play the harmonica.

There was one song that was not a hymn but was based on a gospel song and was my favorite:

Smile a while, and give your face a rest,
Then shake hands with the one you love the best.

When the music ended, we turned to each side, greeting and shaking hands with the people beside us. They always gave us big smiles.

I was alone at the Lanier's home one day when the bell rang. It was a modestly dressed white man who said he was a minister and asked if he could help me or anyone else in the house with any kind of problem, by praying with us. He asked if I had any health problems, and something possessed me to admit that my asthma really bothered me in the Southern climate. He then asked if he could come in and pray to God to send help.

Looking back, I wonder how I let this happen, but I did invite him into the living room. We both knelt on the floor, and he began to pray loudly and intently for Jesus to relieve me of my suffering. He would pause periodically to ask whether I felt any better, and because I hated to let him down I finally said, "Yes, a little bit better." After about a half hour of prayer, he was finished and happy that his pleas had succeeded in at least a partial cure.

I thanked this kind man profusely when he left, and after closing the door behind him, I realized that he was one of the few people I'd ever met who truly was colorblind. He didn't act surprised to see a white woman answering the door in a black neighborhood, and if I were black, he would have offered his prayers and help in the same way. He may not have helped my asthma, but I loved his attitude, generosity and indifference to skin color.

One day when Sib and Johnnie Ruth were the only adults at home, Flap suddenly became quite ill, so much so that it was clear he needed to be seen by a doctor right away. Sib offered to drive Johnnie Ruth and Flap to the emergency room. They quickly got into the car and headed toward the hospital. Suddenly the dreaded Lee Roberts, brother of one of the men involved in the murders of Chaney, Schwerner and Goodman, appeared on his motorcycle and, dressed in his usual tough policeman clothing, pulled Sib over to the side of the road. Sauntering over to the car, Roberts, a snide smile on his face, accused Sib of going through a stop sign (the fake charge often used to harass us) and demanded his driver's license.

Sib denied going through the stop sign and said he had a very sick child in the car who needed to be taken immediately to the emergency room. Ignoring Sib's plea, Roberts began writing out a ticket. When it became clear that Roberts was going to take as long as he could with the ticket, Sib confronted him: "Mr. Roberts, this child is very sick, we can't keep waiting!" Lee just kept laboring over the ticket. There was a pause while Sib thought of what to do next. Then: "Mr. Roberts, this boy is dangerously ill. If anything happens to him, you'll be held personally responsible. I'm going to the hospital now. You need to follow me there if you want to give me a ticket." At that, Sib turned on his engine and started down the road. Surprisingly, Lee Roberts did follow him, most likely because he knew he could get into serious trouble if, in fact, this delay resulted in some real harm to Flap.

The ticket writing process started up again in the hospital parking lot, after Johnnie Ruth and Flap were safely in the emergency room. And that was the end of it, sort of. Flap was given the medicine he needed and recovered quickly. The next day Sib went to the police station to complain of Lee's unconscionable foot-dragging, and the next time we saw Roberts, he was walking his beat, no motorcycle in sight. We liked to think that he was reprimanded for his behavior, his motorcycle taken from him as punishment. We couldn't say for sure, as that kind of satisfaction rarely happened in those days in Mississippi.

A week or so later a brick was thrown through the plate glass window of our office. We told each other it was Roberts who did that, too.

We stayed with Robert Lanier and Johnnie Ruth the whole time we worked in Meridian. I think of them, as well as the other host families, with great gratitude and admiration for their enormous contribution to the Civil Rights struggle.

TEN

REGISTERING VOTERS

I'm gonna' be a registered voter
I'm gonna' be a registered voter one of these days,
Hallelujah
I'm gonna' be a registered voter
Hallelu, hallelu, hallelujah

Verse from "I'm Gonna Sit at the Welcome Table."
Based on the gospel song "I'm Gonna Walk
and Talk with Jesus. "

E ven at ten o'clock in the morning, a blanket of hot, heavy
air sapped our energy as Sib and I stood in front of the
COFO office dressed in jeans and t-shirts. We were waiting
for Sam "Freedom" Brown and Barbara Chaney, the others

who would be joining us that day as we knocked on doors encouraging black Meridians to vote. Although asking people to risk registering to vote was truly the most important activity we could take part in, it tortured me. Knowing the dangers they could well face, I felt inadequate and presumptuous. I felt out of place at each and every doorway I approached.

Posters similar to this, urging black people to vote, were seen in many towns across the Deep South during the Civil Rights struggle.

The proportion of black people registered to vote in Mississippi was miniscule as compared to the proportion of whites. In 1962, the United States Justice Department sued six representative counties in Mississippi over their discriminatory voter registration practices: United States of America v. State of Mississippi et al., Civil Action Number 3312. According to the complaint, the combined white voting age population in the six counties was 53,742, and the number of registered white voters was 38,772. In those same six counties, however, where the combined African American voting age population was 52,558, only 1,955 African Americans were registered. Indeed, in Amite County, 3,295 whites had registered to vote, out of a voting age population of 4,449. Of the 2,560 African Americans of voting age in the county, only one person had managed to register.

Leaning against the small brick COFO storefront, Sib and I waited until the old scuffed up car used by COFO workers pulled up in front of us. We slipped into the back and said our hellos to Sam and Barbara. As we pulled away from the curb, Sam said that we would be going to a neighborhood on the outskirts of the city. It was a neighborhood that I knew. Betty Manuel and a couple of other teenagers who volunteered with us lived there.

We headed down 5th Street and passed through the checkerboard of black and white neighborhoods and then down into a low area called a "bottom" where only black families lived. The irregular dirt roads that linked different parts of the neighborhood were dry and dusty. Behind the worn and sparse front yards, faded and crooked porches fronted most of the houses.

The plan was that I would go with Sam while Sib went with Barbara. That way each pairing would include a black person and a white person. We grabbed our clipboards and agreed to meet back at the car about eleven-thirty to eat our sandwiches and talk over how things were going.

Sam and I were already damp from the heat when we walked up a cracked cement walk to our first front door. Our knock brought hesitant footsteps, and when the door opened part way we faced a man dressed in worn jeans and a plaid shirt who looked to be in his fifties.

Sam spoke first. "Hello, we're from the COFO office on 5th Street. I'm Sam and this is Judy. We're here to talk to you about registering to vote."

"Yes Sir, my name is Alvin." A short awkward pause followed, and the door didn't budge.

I gave it a try. "We're hoping that you and your neighbors will go down to City Hall to register to vote. Mrs. Holly and Mrs. Jackson from just a few streets over went down there last week. Is it OK if we come in and talk to you about it?"

"Yes'm. I know about this. I'm fixin' to go down and register. Y'all don't need to come in. I'm sure to go. I can walk there from here."

Sam's voice was disappointed. "That's great, Alvin. If a lot of black people vote, maybe we can get rid of some bad politicians like Ross Barnett." Barnett was the resolute segregationist governor of Mississippi during the early sixties, and the one that sent the Freedom Riders to Parchman State Penitentiary. He had been quoted as saying: "The good Lord was the original segregationist. He put the black man in Africa . . . He made us white because he wanted us white, and he intended that we should stay that way."

"We need to make some changes around here," Sam continued. "Let us know if you have any questions or need us for anything at all." Sam reached out to give Alvin our contact information.

"Thank you. I'll be sure to go down there," Alvin quickly repeated as we turned to leave. I heard the door shut gently as we reached the end of the path.

I imagined Alvin, grateful to be behind his closed door, heaving a sigh of relief. He knew that if he tried to register his name could appear in the *Meridian Star*, he could be fired from his job, the bank could decide to take away the mortgage on his house. He could be beaten up.

We silently walked to the second house, watching for any sign of a police car or an unknown white person who might be in the neighborhood. We'd had some training. If a policeman found out what we were doing and challenged us, we were to explain that we were just exercising our constitutional rights. If he were to arrest us, maybe that would not be such a bad thing. It could get some publicity that might inspire more action. If a white person were to ask what we were doing on that street, we were to politely answer in the same way. If that person attacked us, we were to lie on the ground in the usual fetal position with our arms protecting our heads and faces.

Our knock at the second house, which looked freshly painted, was answered by a woman dressed in a simple blue dress. We introduced ourselves and she invited us in. Her house was small and neat, the furniture worn but well kept. Family pictures stood on a wooden side table in the living room and there was an open newspaper on the table beside a half-filled cup of coffee.

"I'm Mrs. Johnston," she offered. Smiling, she gestured for us to sit down on the brown couch. It felt to me like she knew exactly who we were. Taking a slow breath, Sam started out again, "We're here to talk to you about registering to vote."

"I know why you're here," she interrupted in a strong, yet friendly voice. "It's no use though. I've been down to City Hall twice now. I've been a teacher for twenty-two years. You'd think they'd know that I'm smart enough to vote." She paused for a minute, tightening her lips and shaking her head. "They'll do anything to keep us black folks from voting. Last time they asked me to explain Article 3, Section 6, Clause 1 of the Mississippi Constitution. Since they wouldn't let me read it, of course I failed the test. They sure don't ask white people those kinds of questions." I sympathized with her. The story wasn't unusual.

"We're trying to get a group of black citizens to go together to City Hall in a group," I explained. "We might be able to get a sympathetic reporter there. Do you think you might consider taking part in that?" Here is where I felt presumptuous; I knew the dangers and so did Mrs. Johnston. Who was I to encourage her to risk so much, I who could go back North, I whose skin color alone gave me more privileges than I could even begin to understand?

Two adults discuss voter registration
with a COFO volunteer in 1964.

But surprisingly, Mrs. Johnston said she just might do it. Sam wrote her name and telephone number on our sheet of paper, and we stayed and chatted for a few minutes, telling Mrs. Johnston about COFO and listening to her angry frustration about the denial of her rights. Before we left, both Sam and I shook her hand and told her that we'd be in touch soon. We both knew that this visit might have been successful but was still a huge question mark.

We had time for one more visit before we met the others for our lunch break. The next house, and the one after that were total losses. Nobody in either one opened their door, though in the front window of the second one I was sure I saw a shadowy movement behind the tattered curtains.

Sam and I walked up to the next home, knocked on the door and waited quietly until we heard footsteps approaching. The door creaked open slowly and revealed a woman with her head held high, wearing gray slacks with a colorful print blouse. She looked at us a bit suspiciously. "What can I do for you?" she inquired in a confident voice. We did the usual explaining, and surprisingly she invited us in. "I appreciate what you all are doing," the woman said, after introducing herself as Mrs. Young. "I'm already a registered voter, and proud of it. It isn't easy for us folks, I'm sure you know. I managed to register a year ago, and guess what my boss at the newspaper said to me when I went to work the next day." Sam and I didn't answer for a few seconds until she continued. "'You're fired!' That's what he said. I've been talking to folks around here. I've been trying to get enough people to go to City Hall for months, but everyone's afraid of getting fired, or even worse. The word got out about me and I had trouble finding a new job, but now at least I've got some work cooking for a white family not too far from here."

Sam and I listened while Mrs. Young continued on about her struggles since she'd registered to vote, how hard it was to make ends meet, how her grown daughter was begging her to stand back and stay out of sight but how she'd never do that. She wanted to be part of the struggle.

When she came to the end of this speech, which seemed to me to have been waiting inside her bursting to be released, Mrs. Young took a deep breath and then quieted down. Although her body relaxed in the big gray easy chair she occupied, her eyes were still bright.

Now it was Sam's turn to tell her about the group we were getting together to go down to City Hall, and though Mrs. Young was already registered, she wanted to just be there, to swell the crowd and boost the morale. We took her name and number and I became excited, and as my spirits lifted to match hers, I wanted to throw my arms around this woman. I walked toward her and, as if she knew exactly what was going on in me, she opened her arms.

As Sam and I headed down Mrs. Young's walk and toward the COFO car, we glanced at each other, each of us with a small smile matching the hope we felt. Would all this effort, all this walking, all this talking, all this gathering oneself against the fear we felt pressing around us really bring about a change? Would all those with black skin ever be seen as equal to those whose DNA left their skin a lighter color?

Sam and I walked toward Barbara and Sib. Maybe if each person had a little hope it would amount to one big hope. Maybe if all of us brought forward whatever courage we could muster, our combined efforts would awaken enough daring in enough hearts to challenge the way things had been for so many centuries.

ELEVEN

PICKETING THE LAMAR AND PAYING THE PRICE

Woke up this mornin' with my mind stayed on freedom
Oh, woke up this mornin' with my mind stayed on freedom
Woke up this mornin' with my mind stayed on freedom
Hallelu, Hallelu, Hallelujah.

Verse from "Woke Up This Mornin'
with my Mind Stayed on Freedom."
Based on the gospel song "Woke Up This Mornin'
with My Mind Stayed on Jesus."

The weather was about as chilly as it gets during a Mississippi winter, cold enough for Sib and me to wear coats as we walked past the run-down storefronts on 5th

Street. Down a side street we could see City Hall with its two sets of broad steps leading up to the huge concrete platform fronting the entrance. That was where, the week before, we picketed in protest of the many bureaucratic tricks used to prevent black citizens from voting. The most common practice was to ask black applicants to recite, word for word, obscure passages of the Mississippi State Constitution.

Practicing for the Lamar Hotel picket line inside the COFO office.

As we passed under the faded red awning of the little breakfast and lunch place where we often ate, Lee Roberts, the brother of one of the Klansmen charged with the Neshoba County murders, slowed down his huge policeman's motorcycle to check us out. We kept our eyes straight ahead, and he decided to pass us by this time. It was at times like this that I became acutely aware of how black people must always feel when in the presence of police: they were the subjugated "other" and always in danger.

Arriving at the office, we found Mrs. Crowell, Sam Brown, Eric Weinberger, and a dozen or more other volunteers there. Our job that day was to rehearse our plan to picket the Lamar Hotel in downtown Meridian. The policy at the Lamar, like at so many other places, was to deny employment to black people.

In the back corner of the crowded office was an old wooden table set up with materials needed to make the placards we would carry, each one large enough to cover our bodies from chest to knees. Sitting down on the worn gray and white checked linoleum floor, I wrote out my message:

WE'VE COME TOO FAR TO COME
TO A SEGREGATED HOTEL!

Mrs. Crowell's slogan was:

LAMAR HOTEL MENU:
JIM CROW

When we finished, Eric called us all together and had us walk, signs around our necks, in the tight circle dictated by our small and cramped office space. Eric kept up a running commentary: "Remember, we are all committed to nonviolence. If anyone yells at you, spits on you or shoves you, remain calm and don't retaliate. If you are actually attacked, remember the defensive position we've rehearsed: down on the ground in a fetal position, knees pulled up to protect your gut, elbows bent over your face." By now this was almost routine.

The next day Sib and I followed the same route to our office and joined the other volunteers. We were all very quiet as we walked together down 5th Street and around the corner to the wide sidewalk in front of the Lamar Hotel. Once there we made our circle before the Lamar's front entrance, about six or seven feet from each other. It was a simple thing to do, and I wasn't too nervous or afraid. I had hung my sign around my neck and was ready for the hours ahead.

But even before any angry crowd had time to gather, I glanced to the side and saw police approaching. If I felt I had been ready, I was wrong. I thought I was about to be arrested again and I didn't think I could face it. I looked around for a way to escape, but nobody else was doing that. They were all bravely staying in the picket line. My fear embarrassed me. How could I face the humiliation of walking away while my husband and friends were hauled off to jail?

So I stayed.

The police ripped our signs away and had us wait to be picked up. Once we were inside the paddy wagon, "We Shall Overcome" burst forth and rocked the wagon all the way to the police station. It turned out that the county jail had cells only for black men, white men, and black women. Since I was the only white woman on the picket line that day, I would have to be by myself in a cell in the police station.

I was devastated. I didn't think I could endure jail on my own without the support of other people. I had heard too many stories of white Civil Rights advocates being beaten up by other white prisoners while behind bars. How long would I be held? Would I be attacked? Would I be sent back to Parchman? Would my medication be taken away again?

Before long, a policeman came to escort me down a long bleak corridor to a cell. The good news was that no one else was in it; the bad news was that I was alone. The walls were plain concrete with only a single high barred window at the back. Against one wall, several feet back from where the prison bars separated me from the corridor, stood a cot. I lay down with my fears.

Soon I could hear the men, who had been put in a separate cell while waiting to be taken to the county jail, begin to sing Carver Neblett's song.

If you miss me from the back of the bus
And you can't find me nowhere
Come on up to the front of the bus
And I'll be riding up there.

I could just picture Sam "Freedom" Brown clapping and keeping time with his whole body . . . from his head to his feet . . . and I began to smile, and then to laugh . . . and then I began to sing too.

Before a lot of time passed, I heard noise down the corridor and immediately afterward saw the men being taken to the county jail. Joe Morse said, "I feel that I have been unjustly arrested and refuse to cooperate in any way." Then he fell to the floor, showing his resistance by going limp. Sib followed, and then Greg Kaslo and the others. One of them yelled out "I want to join my friends." It was hard to watch them being dragged by my cell. Lee Roberts made sure that, on the way, the bodies of the men were slammed against the steel lockers along the corridor.

Eric Weinberger, one of our co-workers, came to visit me later and brought me cigarettes. I felt awful having any fears when I thought about what Eric had been through. His whole back was scarred from electric cow prodders used to punish him for his civil rights activities. Once he was picked up by his groin and swung around. He seemed very pessimistic and withdrawn.

As evening approached I began to have more visitors. Lee Roberts came by with several women, one by one. They stood there in their tight pedal pushers, dangly earrings, high heels, and well-kept hair and stared into my cell. Lee Roberts said things like "Can you believe it?" or "That's the white woman." or "She sure has big feet doesn't she." while peals of laughter came from the women. Other men came by with similarly dressed women and called me a "n—— lover" and a "stubborn bitch," all accompanied by giggles and laughter from their "proper" companions. Another woman yelled, "Go back home! We all know you only came here to fuck n—— s."

Two teenaged girls came by. One asked me why I hung around with n——s. I said that I didn't run around like she thought, that I only believed they should be treated like I was. The other girl said, "Oh yeah, well why did God make them inferior, and why did he make them slaves?" I told her that God didn't make them slaves; men made them slaves. Then she wanted to know why we didn't just leave the n——s alone. They were happy. So I answered, "If they're so happy, why did they all protest today?" She got quite aggravated at this and stated, "You know that every one of them arrested is from the North." When I told her that wasn't so, most of them were from Mississippi, her reply was, "Well, I guess that there are lowdown whites as well as lowdown n——s." They left, but came back in five minutes with Lee Roberts and told him that I was from Boston and loved n——s. Then they all went away laughing.

Nonviolence was easy during all these visits. I was scared and sometimes had no idea what to say. I was appalled and knew I couldn't begin to defend myself or the Movement to people like that. It was awkward, stressful and discouraging to maintain silence and a proud demeanor, sitting on the cot, my stomach tied up in knots.

A few hours later an elderly white man dressed in saggy gray pants and a faded shirt came to my cell. He had a quiet manner and approached me shyly. He had apparently gone out, bought a chicken dinner and graciously offered it to me. His brave gesture touched me deeply, and I took the meal with great thanks. I never did learn whether he worked at the police station or had just somehow gotten in.

But I couldn't help thinking about what might happen next and my stomach was too upset to even think about eating.

At some point I fell into a restless and anxious sleep. When I woke up the next morning a policeman came to get me. "You're free," he announced, "One of those lawyers came here and got you out." Shocked at this unexpected gift of release, I followed the policeman from my cell and saw that Sib and the others who had gone to the county jail, were already back at the police station. Joe's shirt was so torn that it was practically falling off him.

We were allowed to walk away with the lawyer who had freed us. He was one of a handful of courageous Civil Rights attorneys, black and white, who crisscrossed the Deep South in those days, heading to where there was trouble and using their skills to deal with it the best they could. Inspired by them, Sib decided to go to law school when we left the South.

On the way back to the COFO office, Sib told me his story. Crammed into the paddy wagon taking the men to the county jail, they decided to lock arms tightly as they were brought into the building so that they just might be able to all be detained up in the safety of the black prisoners' holding tank. The white prisoners' tank was on the second floor, the black tank on the third. A narrow spiral staircase connected the first, second, and third floors, and in the confusion the chain of men managed to get on the stairs and past the second floor.

Sib, however, was the last link in the chain. Two cops tore him loose and dragged him back to the second floor tank.

There he was, alone with a bunch of white locals. He sat at a table with his head down, pretending to be drunk, and eventually fell asleep there. Miraculously, none of the other prisoners paid any attention to him; most of them were drunk, too.

I don't remember our lawyer's name or on what grounds he managed to get us out. But I do remember hugging Sib and all my friends and feeling light as a feather as we all broke into freedom songs to celebrate our release.

My insides relaxed, but it was still two days before I was able to eat again.

TWELVE
VISITING HARRIS HIGH SCHOOL

Black and white together, we shall not be moved
Black and white together, we shall not be moved
Just like a tree that's standing by the water
We shall not be moved.

Verse from "We Shall Not Be Moved."
Based on folk songs going back to slave times
and often used as a union protest song.
This was often sung by Pete Seeger as a protest.

In the spring of 1965 I left the COFO office with Nancy, a tall, bright, but somewhat awkward black high school student. She was one of the teenagers who often hung out at our office and who took part in some of the activities we organized, such as sit-ins and voting registration drives. She also attended our Freedom School regularly.

The two of us had an appointment with Mr. Barton, principal of Harris High, the local segregated high school for blacks. We hoped to change his negative attitude toward the Civil Rights activities going on in Meridian.

I wore a simple blue skirt and a short-sleeved white blouse. I had put on my very best shoes, the usual worn black sandals. Nancy wore a simple print summer dress with a plain white shirt over it.

The weather was perfect, warm and sunny. But my hands were cold. As Nancy and I went up the wide cement steps and approached the large square brick building, we shared a quick glance, half anxiety and half mutual support. We knew that Mr. Barton, though black, did not openly support Civil Rights activity. Among other things, he threatened students who were participating in our Freedom School program, including Nancy, with expulsion. We planned to talk to him about what was taught in Freedom School: history, biology, English, and yes, black studies. We hoped to change his attitude toward it.

Mr. Barton had been at Harris High for about thirty years, and had originally been appointed by an all-white board of education. He only hired teachers who had a generous attitude toward whites and he insisted that they not participate in Civil Rights activities. In the 1964 presidential election, he had supported Barry Goldwater despite Goldwater's resistance to any Civil Rights reform. He suspended students who wore LBJ buttons.

It was heartbreaking and demoralizing to realize that a person with such power, who was a leader in the black community, and who had so much influence over teenagers, refused to take a stand for his people.

I was torn between my anger at him and my knowledge that being against the system was easy for me, but enormously difficult for him. What would our conversation be like? Would we be able to say the right things? Was I, a white woman from the North, the right person to be accompanying Nancy on this delicate mission? And if I was anxious, how must Nancy feel? She was only eighteen, and her principal was already ill disposed toward her.

As we entered the building Nancy turned to me and, with a small self-deprecating expression on her face, said, "I'm nervous."

"I know," I answered. "I am too."

We found our way through the institutional corridors to the principal's office and quietly knocked on the door. Mr. Barton, dressed in a gray business suit and a white shirt and tie, his shoes brightly polished, met us with a big smile. "How you doin' today? Come right on in."

Nancy and I sat down on two wooden chairs facing him across his huge metal desk. We chatted with him somewhat stiltedly about not much of anything for a while, until I began to feel tense. I knew that I had to turn the conversation toward more important things. Eventually I brought up a short article that had been in the *Meridian Star* about black people who had attempted to register to vote, names and all. Because the literacy test was administered so unfairly, almost all black people failed. If that weren't enough, publishing their names could lead to dire consequences. In other words, those in power were not only going to rig the test but punish potential black voters for even trying. I asked Mr. Barton what he thought of the article.

It hadn't occurred to me that the principal of a high school wouldn't be in favor of fairness in voter registration procedures, so I was shocked when he looked away from us and hesitated quite a while. "Well," he finally said, "I think it's a good thing to have the voter registration test. It's important to have only intelligent and educated people vote in a democracy."

"But many black people who get turned down are smarter than the whites who pass with no trouble," Nancy tried to reason. "That test is just rigged to keep the black community from having any power." Her voice was calm, but her arms were crossed and her one visible hand was gripping her other arm tightly. She held her head high. "I'm really sorry to disagree with you, Mr. Barton, but I see a lot of ways that the voting registration system here intimidates black people. We're asked to recite, from memory and word for word, whole sections of the Mississippi Constitution. There are long, long delays to even find out about the test and its results."

I looked at Nancy, amazed at her courage in confronting her principal so directly. I doubted whether I could have done it myself.

"I don't see any voting intimidation in Meridian," Mr. Barton answered, looking right at us. He leaned back in his chair, with one ankle resting on the other knee. I briefly slid my eyes toward Nancy and saw her sneak a look at me. "And these voting rights demonstrations," Mr. Barton continued. "It just makes me sick to turn on the TV and see what's been going on in Selma. One hundred demonstrations won't teach you as much as one day in the classroom!"

What use was there in more talk? Mr. Barton was clearly determined as steel, at least outwardly, to defend the white power structure. But just because we couldn't let the Freedom School issue completely go, I asked him whether he would reconsider his attitude about it. Would he allow the students to make up their own minds about whether to take part in Civil Rights activities? Would he let them decide whether they would join our after school program to learn more about regular school subjects and black history?

"These students should be paying attention to their high school work, not wasting their time sitting at lunch counters. *That's* how they'll get ahead in their lives," was his authoritarian answer. "We teach them all the subjects they need right here."

I could guess at what some of the reasons might be for Mr. Barton's frustrating mind-set. It was hard not to think that he was protecting himself and his position; but it was also possible he wanted to protect his school and his students from having funds cut off. It could easily be just plain fear of white people's response to him. Whatever the source of his willful blindness to racism, we were not going to change his mind.

Nancy and I had remained polite during the visit. It would only make things worse if we had confronted him with anger. He might even clamp down more seriously than ever on the students.

Mr. Barton did, however, invite us on a tour of the school. It had been renovated a while ago, so was in reasonable shape. We visited a history class and I found it even more depressing than I had expected. The students were just lectured about World War II, and, never encouraged to enter the discussion, they were bored and restless. Someone lent me a textbook, and as I thumbed through it I failed to see even one photo which included black soldiers from this country. Neither the book nor the teacher mentioned the part black soldiers played in the war, or President Truman's desegregation of the United States Army. Only at the Freedom School were students helped to reclaim their own history.

We shook hands with Mr. Barton and said our good-byes courteously as we left. After we closed the door behind us, the corners of Nancy's mouth turned down as she shook her head sadly. Our eyes met again as I put my arm around her shoulders. At one point she said, "Can you believe he said those things, Judy?" I had no answer. We walked back to the COFO office side by side, and in silence.

THIRTEEN

THE POWER OF SONG

We shall overcome
We shall overcome
We shall overcome some day.
Oh, deep in my heart, I do believe
We shall overcome some day.

Verse from "We Shall Overcome."
Based on a gospel song.

Music was the heartbeat of the Civil Rights Movement
in the South. Most of the songs we sang were derived
from age-old Negro spirituals, but newer words were often
added to fit the circumstances. We sang these songs to give
us courage when we were afraid; we sang them to strengthen

ourselves; we sang because it united us, though sometimes we hardly knew the person singing next to us. We sang when we were hopeful, and when we were grieving.

Student protestors singing in front of the bus they would take to Mississippi to volunteer in COFO activities.

I was always overwhelmed by the power of these songs, just as I was when I joined in singing them the first time in that small church in Birmingham, Alabama.

Ain't gonna' let nobody turn me round,
Turn me 'round
Turn me 'round
Ain't gonna' let nobody turn me 'round
I'm gonna' keep on a'walkin'
Keep on a'talkin'
Walkin' on to freedom's land

During my time in Mississippi, I sang these songs and others many, many times with my co-workers in meetings held in churches, on sidewalk picket lines, and in Freedom School. I sang them with my fellow Civil Rights prisoners on the way from the Jackson City Jail to Parchman State Penitentiary. And once there, in our cells, we all sang out, black and white women together, rocking the prison walls to show the jailers that they could imprison our bodies, but never our minds and souls. It was the singing that propped up my spirits and made me feel strong. It was singing that pushed aside my isolation when I was in a tiny cell by myself.

I once sang songs of freedom to pass the time with a carload of people on a long ride from Meridian to New Orleans, past swamps and houses on stilts. We were headed for a COFO conference during which I heard the announcement of Malcolm X's tragic assassination. Malcolm X was a black Muslim minister who fought fiercely for African American rights and felt rage at the white community for what they had done and were still doing to black Americans. Many people admired him, but those who did not accused him of inciting violence and reverse racism. The words of his death struck me like a blow and I sat in my seat almost unable to move. I had heard Malcolm X speak several times in Boston and New York, and was always deeply impressed and moved by him. But I was shocked when I heard barely any groans or "Oh No's" in the large meeting hall. Only a tiny moment of silence and then on with the business of the meeting. I wondered if it was our commitment to nonviolence that kept people from feeling kinship with Malcolm X or grief at his loss. I don't think he was a violent man, but his rhetoric was more of anger than of love.

The meeting went on and soon we would be leaving. It was time to get up and sing. It felt good to reach out for the hands beside me, to let our freedom songs remind me again that we were all working toward the same goal. We were united in that, and we could put our differences aside.

Oh freedom, Oh freedom
Oh freedom over me
And before I'd be a slave
I'll be buried in my grave
And go home to my Lord and be free

—Verse from "Oh Freedom," based on a post-Civil War African American Freedom Song.

Luke told me, in a letter, about the day of James Chaney's funeral in Meridian, which took place before Sib and I arrived there. As people wound their way down streets from all corners of the city to join in the funeral march to the church, the words to "We Shall Overcome" rang out everywhere. It was a promise to James Chaney that his work would continue.

I believe that the music of the Movement enabled us to maintain the nonviolent stance that helped move us forward. It was easier not to fight back and to preserve our dignity when we were as one with others in deeply felt song. The music kept our minds on what we were striving for and the path to get there. It created an immediate and almost physical connection with the people we supported and who supported us.

I always felt privileged to be part of the Movement, but never as much as when we were all bound together in its music. Everyone knew the songs. They were our hymns. I could be somewhere with any number of people I'd never met before, and the music would make us all one.

"We Shall Overcome" was the most beloved and famous anthem of the Movement. The words and music said it all. The words are full of hope, yet the melody speaks of enormous sadness.

The second verse is:

We'll walk hand in hand,
We'll walk hand in hand,
We'll walk hand in hand some day.
Oh, deep in my heart, I do believe
We'll walk hand in hand some day.

FOURTEEN

WITNESSING JOHN DOAR
AND THE VOTING RIGHTS HEARING

We're marching on to freedom land
We're marching on to freedom land
God's our strength from day to day
As we walk the narrow way
We're going forward
We're going forward
One day we're gonna' be free.

Verse from "We're Marching on to Freedom Land."

"We're Marching on to Freedom Land"
may be an adaptation of the gospel song
"We're Marching to Zion." In this civil rights adaptation,
"the narrow way" means the difficulties people face who are
working to get "freedom for all."

John Doar (right) with James Meredith, a twenty-nine-year-old veteran who decided in 1961 to apply to the then segregated University of Mississippi.

On an early morning in 1965, Sib and I and some others left the COFO office to attend one of the evidentiary hearings in the case of United States vs. the State of Mississippi. John Doar, Assistant U.S. Attorney General for Civil Rights from 1960 to 1967, was taking evidence all over the Deep South showing that the civil rights of black citizens were being systematically violated by the states.

Today the hearing was to be in Meridian and there was no way we intended to miss it.

John Doar, a true hero of the Movement, was involved in several of the most important and significant Civil Rights cases during the sixties. He helped protect the Freedom Riders. He prosecuted the federal case against the murderers of Michael Schwerner, James Chaney, and Andrew Goodman. When the four-day, fifty-four-mile march for voting rights took place from Selma to Montgomery, Alabama in March of 1965, he walked one half block ahead of the thousands of demonstrators to represent the United States Department of Justice. John Doar helped draft the Voting Rights Act of August 1965 signed by President Lyndon B. Johnson, at last enforcing voting rights for all Americans.

James Meredith, shown on the preceding page with John Doar, was twice refused admission to the University of Mississippi because of his race. In 1962, the district court ordered that Meredith be admitted, and it was John Doar who represented Meredith in the struggle that followed. Ross Barnett, then governor of Alabama, had stated, "No school in Mississippi will be integrated while I am your governor." Attorney General Robert F. Kennedy then ordered 500 U.S. Marshals to accompany Meredith during his arrival and registration at the university. When angry white mobs gathered, Kennedy had to call in the Mississippi National Guard as well as Federal troops before Meredith could start classes.

Sib and I were incredibly excited at the prospect of witnessing one of John Doar's hearings. We wanted to be there as he presented the evidence that would show beyond any doubt that black people were being denied their right to vote. It was clear that if you didn't have the power of the vote, you had no power at all. We all hoped this might be the long awaited and historic case that gave blacks the same right to register and vote that had been granted to white people so long ago. I learned from our voter registration drive that many potential black voters were willing to brave white retaliation, but stayed home. They knew they would be deemed illiterate at City Hall because of their inability to recite and interpret an obscure and arcane provision of the Mississippi Constitution. In the meantime, of course, white registrants had no such burden. If the playing field could only be leveled, perhaps our hard work might really pay off.

We walked up the broad marble steps to the Federal District Courthouse, through an imposing entrance and into a small courtroom where quite a few onlookers and witnesses, both black and white, were already seated. The hearing hadn't started yet and murmured conversations filled the air. This was the big day, and none of us knew what to expect.

Finding a long bench not too far from the front, our group filed in and sat down quietly. Before us and on the other side of a polished wooden balustrade were two large wooden tables. At the one on the left were seated six white lawyers representing the state of Mississippi and various county registrars, all of them relaxed, slouched and chatting with a confident air. The table itself was cluttered with piles of massively thick law books and scattered papers: it was a crowded and busy tableau.

At the table on my right a lone tall white lawyer in a dark suit sat quietly with his hands folded calmly in front of him. His table was bare . . . no books, no papers, no associates. This was John Doar.

In those days there were two federal district court judges sitting in Meridian, Judge Mize and Judge Cox. Both were segregationists, but Judge Cox was a real KKK type. Sure enough it was Judge Cox who came out of chambers wearing his dark robe and already looking angry. When he banged his gavel sharply on his bench and called the court to order, the murmuring died down and the room fell into silence.

After all these years, I have no specific memory of the exact words used by Mr. Doar's witnesses. The testimony of William Ray and Ramie Dennis (fictional names) is taken verbatim from various depositions in this case: <u>United States of America vs. State of Mississippi, et. al., Civil Action No. 3312</u>. The testimony of Dorothy Manuel, another fictional name, represents the general nature of the story told by the many black witnesses called by Mr. Doar. She may be a fiction, but the experiences she describes are not. What follows are excerpts from the depositions.

After the opening formalities John Doar stood up and called his first witness.

"Will Mr. William Ray please take the stand."

A white man looking to be about twenty-five, wearing jeans and a faded plaid shirt, stood up, walked past the onlookers and took the witness stand. He leaned to the side in his chair, supporting his head with his left hand.

Q: "Would you tell us your full name, Mr. Ray?"

A: "William Ray."

Q: "And where do you live?"

A: "Meridian, Mississippi."

Q: "What do you do there?"

A: "I drive a truck."

Q: "Mr. Ray, are you registered to vote?"

A: "Yes, sir."

Q: "Mr. Ray, how far did you go in school?"

A: "Well, not too far, about in one door and out the other."

Q: "Did you go to the first grade?"

Suddenly one of the lawyers at the defense table jumped up, holding a sheaf of papers in one hand and clamoring for attention. Looking at the judge he shouted, "We object to this question and all other questions about this witness's qualifications to vote. Since he is already registered, any questions along this line would be immaterial and incompetent."

Judge Cox, looking extremely pained, overruled the objection. He might have been an ardent segregationist, but the last thing he wanted was to be reversed on appeal for upholding patently frivolous objections. John Doar continued his line of questioning.

Q: "Mr. Ray, do you read and write, sir?"

A: "I can kind of scribble my name. I can't read to do no good."

Q: "Mr. Ray, I would like to read out loud to you a section from the Constitution of the State of Mississippi and I would like you to tell me what it means. Here is what it says: 'All elections by the people shall be by ballot.' Would you like to tell the court what it means? Mr. Ray?"

A: "No I wouldn't care to."

Q: "Mr. Ray, you are of the white race, is that correct?"

A: "Yes, sir."

John Doar: "That's all for this witness, your honor."

None of the defense attorneys attempted to cross-examine Mr. Ray. It was clear that any questioning would just make matters worse for the State of Mississippi. This strategy was repeated throughout the hearing; the idea was to minimize damage by getting white witnesses off the stand as quickly as possible.

A rustle of low murmurs seeped into the air as William Ray left the witness stand and went back to his seat. I looked at Sib, rolling my eyes and shrugging my shoulders in amazement. John Doar had folded himself back into his chair but the judge immediately announced, "Call your next witness, Mr. Doar." Ramie Dennis was called to the stand.

Q: "Would you please state your full name."

A: "Ramie Dennis."

Q: "How old are you?"

A: "Twenty-six."

Q: "How far did you go in school?"

A: "I don't know. I don't remember."

Q: "Did you go to school?"

A: "I think so."

Q: "Did you go to the first grade, Mr. Dennis?"

A: "I don't remember."

Q: "Did you graduate from high school, Mr. Dennis?"

A: "I don't remember."

Q: "What do you do for a living?"

A: "Farm."

Q: "Are you registered to vote?"

A: "Yes, sir."

Q: "Was there anyone else in the room when you were filling out the voter registration form?"

A: "Just the man in charge of it."

Q: "Do you remember doing anything besides signing your name in the book in order to register to vote?"

A: "I don't remember."

Q: "Were you required to copy and interpret any part of the Constitution of the State of Mississippi?"

A: "I don't remember."

Q: "Mr. Dennis, can you read and write?"

A: (No answer.)

Q: "Mr. Dennis, I show you a copy of the Constitution of the State of Mississippi and ask you to read Section 30."

"Objection!" came again from the crowded defense table. "We request the witness not to answer as again, this question is incompetent and immaterial."

Once more Judge Cox overruled the objection, looking even more upset and now angry as well, angry that he found himself playing a role in a case headed toward radically changing the complexion of Mississippi's electorate.

Q: "Mr. Dennis, will you read Section 30?"

A: "I'd rather not."

Q: "Mr. Dennis, can you read and write?"

A: "A little."

Q: "Mr. Dennis, you are white, are you not?"

A: "Sir?"

Q: "I say, you are a member of the white race, aren't you?"

A: "Umnhmn, yes sir."

Joan Doar: "That's all."

Once again the defense declined to cross examine and Mr. Dennis was excused. The soft buzz of low voices filled the courtroom. The lawyers at the defense table were leaning in toward each other and speaking intently. John Doar sat quite serenely, looking out the window with his hands again folded, waiting to be directed to call his next witness.

"Will Dorothy Manuel please take the stand."

A black woman looking to be in her mid-thirties and wearing a simple blue and white print dress walked up and took her seat in the witness box.

Q: "Would you please state your full name."

A: "Dorothy Manuel, sir."

Q: "How old are you?"

A: "Thirty-nine, sir."

Q: "What kind of work do you do?"

A: "I'm a high school English teacher, sir."

Q: "How far did you go in school, Mrs. Manuel?"

A: "I finished high school and went to teacher's college."

Q: "Are you registered to vote?"

A: "No, sir."

Q: "Have you attempted to register?"

A: "Yes, sir."

Q: "What happened?"

A: "The registrar took out the Constitution of the State of Mississippi and without showing it to me, asked me to repeat Article 3 of Section 30 word for word to him. I generally know what Article 3 is about, but I was unable to do that."

Q: "Did the registrar show Section 30 to you and ask you to read and interpret it?"

A: "No, sir. He just said that I didn't pass the test."

Q: "Mrs. Manuel, you are of the Negro race, are you not?"

A: "Yes, sir. I am a black woman."

Q: "Were you threatened in any way when you went to register to vote?"

A: "Yes, sir. My name was published in the local paper and I was fired from the part-time job I had then, working at Mr. Hughes' book store."

The hearing followed along these lines for several hours. Mr. Doar called at least a dozen witnesses, black professionals who had failed the literacy test sandwiched between illiterate whites who had done just fine.

When Judge Cox called an end to the hearing we stood up and headed toward the exit. I did my best to look solemn and dignified, while inside I wanted to jump up and down. If all the other hearings were like the one I just witnessed, there would certainly be a ruling—if not by Judge Cox, then by a higher court—that the voting rights of black people were systematically being denied in the state of Mississippi. Grabbing Sib's hand as we left the building, I looked up and saw he had a huge smile on his face. I let go of decorum and matched it.

FIFTEEN

MARCHING FROM SELMA TO MONTGOMERY

I'm on my way
And I won't turn back
I'm on my way
Oh, and I won't turn back
I'm on my way
Mmm I won't turn back
I'm on my way
Praise god
I'm on my way.

Verse from "I'm on My Way to Canaan Land."
Adapted from a gospel song.

To our disappointment but not surprise, John Doar's lawsuit was tossed out by Judge Cox. But this was all part of the strategy: to bring cases against voting registrars throughout the South, to lose before most (if not all) of the district courts, to pursue all necessary appeals and finally get before the Supreme Court, where for the first time the literacy test would be scrutinized by fair-minded judges.

In the meantime street protests continued, and took on such strength that in Selma, Alabama over 3,000 people had been arrested for demonstrating against voter discrimination.

As tensions rose in Selma, the SCLC (the Southern Christina Leadership Conference, Martin Luther King Jr.'s organization) and SNCC (the Student Nonviolent Coordinating Committee) decided to organize a fifty-four mile march from Selma to Montgomery, the capitol of Alabama, to dramatize the unconscionable and often brutal methods used by the white Southern establishment to keep black citizens from voting.

At that time I was back home in Massachusetts taking a break because of my asthma, which was always much worse in the South. Sib, however, busy with a project in Meridian, stayed behind.

On the night of March 7th, 1965, I was in my parents' home, watching TV footage of eight hundred marchers, just as they arrived at the Edmond Pettis Bridge on the edge of Selma. They were attacked with tear gas and clubs by Alabama State Troopers, some on horseback, as well as a mob of white men.

I sat with my hand over my mouth, horrified by the hatred, violence, and blood I was seeing in what was later called Bloody Sunday. The marchers had no choice but to turn back.

Marchers being attacked by State Troopers and other white citizens on Bloody Sunday. On the ground to the right is John Lewis, later to become a United States Representative.

Later that night I got a call from Sib, letting me know that a second March was being planned for March 9th, and that he and a few others were leaving for Selma the next morning. He said that their mood was one of exhilaration; they were about to take part in what was clearly going to be a huge and historic Civil Rights event. He reassured me that, because of the publicity generated by Sunday's violence, many reporters and TV cameramen were expected to be there this next time, compelling Selma officials to do everything they could to prevent more bloodshed. I felt terrible that I had deserted the Movement just when as many people as possible were needed to demonstrate for the right to vote. I wanted to be there! But at least Sib was going to be able take part in this tremendously important event.

Two nights later I watched the news again. Two thousand people were in Selma for this second attempt to reach Montgomery. They were singing and carrying a huge banner proclaiming, "We Shall Overcome" at the head of the March. Many of them held flags or signs saying "End Terror in Selma," "We Want Our Vote Now," and "We March with Selma." Young and old held them, black and white held them. Nuns and businessmen held them. It looked like nothing could stop them.

I scoured the television screen hoping to catch sight of Sib, but had no luck.

It was not long before the March reached the Edmund Pettis Bridge, where the brutal beatings had taken place on Bloody Sunday. When Martin Luther King, leading the March, reached the top of the rise in the bridge and began to descend the other side he saw a large police cordon, several officers deep, facing the March and blocking the road. Behind them were officers on horseback. All wore helmets and were armed with clubs. There was nothing in their attitude or their deployment to indicate that the March was going much further. The troopers were again ready to attack, rather than protect, the nonviolent demonstrators.

Faced with this barrier, Reverend King asked for permission from the police to pray. Cameras showed him and others near the front of the March kneeling in the street, heads bowed, facing the officers.

King decided, rather than to risk another Bloody Sunday, to turn around a second time. They would try again a few days later, once they got an anticipated federal injunction prohibiting the city and state from attacking participants or otherwise interfering with the March to Montgomery.

The injunction was issued a week later. When George Wallace, the governor of Alabama, agreed to let the March take place but refused to guarantee the safety of the marchers, President Johnson federalized the Alabama National Guard, and on March 21, thousands of people left Selma for the third and final March to Montgomery. Many thousands more joined them on their way to the State Capitol, and on March 25th, the news showed twenty-five thousand people entering Montgomery, singing, clapping, and waving flags demanding voting rights for all people.

By that point Sib and the others from Meridian, sorry to not to be able to wait for the injunction, had left, as they were needed at their COFO office for the important work that was going on there.

Tragically, missing from this triumphal crowd would be Jimmy Lee Jackson, a black teenager shot and killed by police during one of the earlier Selma demonstrations, and Reverend James Reeb, who had come from Massachusetts to join in the protest. He was ambushed the night before the second attempt to reach Montgomery and beaten to death by a group of white thugs. Adding to that toll, Viola Liuzzo, a white volunteer from Michigan, was shot and killed by members of the Ku Klux Klan while driving marchers to the Montgomery airport at the conclusion of the March. Jimmie Lee Jackson's killer was not tried and convicted until 45 years later. Reverend Reeb's killers were apprehended and tried for murder. Three were acquitted and the fourth fled to Mississippi where the authorities there refused to return him for trial. Of the two Klan members whom the state accused of killing Viola Liuzzo, one died of a heart attack before trial, while the other was acquitted. He was, however, convicted later in federal court of a civil rights violation and served six years in jail.

As a result of the Selma demonstrations, Bloody Sunday, the successful March to Montgomery and the murders, together with the evidence gathered by John Doar, President Johnson successfully prevailed on Congress to pass the Voting Rights Act of 1965. Literacy tests were prohibited and Southern states were put on probation until blacks were registered in numbers proportionate to their population. During this probationary period no changes in voter qualifications could be made without the prior approval of the United States Justice Department.

Martin Luther King Jr. said that the March from Selma to Montgomery was a shining moment in the conscience of our country. It was certainly one of the greatest achievements of the Civil Rights Movement; without it, who knows how long it would have taken for the black citizens of the South to finally participate in our democracy.

EPILOGUE

NO, IT'S NOT OVER

We have hung our heads and cried
For all those like Martin who died
They died for us and they died for me
They died for the cause of Liberty
But we'll never turn back
No we'll never turn back
Until we've all been free
And we have equality.

Verse from "We'll Never Turn Back."
Based on the spiritual "We've Been 'Buked
and We've Been Scorned."

When it came time for us to leave in the late summer of 1965, it was not easy. Despite the hardships and fear involved, I loved being part of the struggle and the excitement of life working with others to change, little by little, the status quo. How would I feel when I woke up at home? How would I fill my need to know that each day I was working toward a meaningful goal? What would happen to the friends with whom I had walked the picket lines and insisted on service at segregated counters?

In the South, I had learned a great deal that I would carry with me for the rest of my life. I always knew that, since they were first brought here as slaves, black people in this country had been faced with enormous prejudice, injustice and violence. It was only in Mississippi, however, that I got the enormity of what they were still dealing with, to say nothing of the equal enormity of its converse: the advantages and privileges white people take for granted as their rightful due. When I sat with my black co-workers at segregated lunch counters, never being served, it was easy for me. I am white and I could go home and be accepted as an equal at any time. For the black people sitting with me, the story was different. Most of them lived in Meridian where they were known, watched, and in danger. Leaving was extremely daunting for them, and in most cases, not what they wanted to do. And even if they did leave, they would always be judged by the color of their skin.

During the Civil Rights Movement I began to see myself as a fighter for change, as an individual who, along with others, could make a difference in the world. Protest had become part of who I was, and I would carry that part of me wherever I went.

Back home there were plenty of issues that cried out for action. The unjust war in Vietnam dominated the 1960's. The Women's Movement was beginning to take on the power that would influence the lives of all people in my generation, our children, and our children's children. And later, the AIDS epidemic hit the already misunderstood and reviled gay community with a devastating blow. The organized response to each of these issues had a place for me to push for what I believed in.

I think back to when I was a teenager and wanted so much to make my life meaningful, and I feel gratitude for the time I spent in the Civil Rights Movement. It taught me how to take an active stand against injustice and added a great deal of depth and meaning to the months and years following my days in Mississippi.

The Movement did succeed in defeating racism supported by local laws and elected officials in the Deep South. Jim Crow hotels, restaurants, buses, theaters, waiting rooms, restrooms and water fountains are a thing of the past, and of most importance, the unimpeded right to vote is now ensured by federal law. I thrill to see African Americans creating role models for our young people. Not only have we had an African American president, but we see African Americans as news anchors on television, to say nothing of their being omnipresent in its commercials. They serve in Congress, they are governors, mayors, municipal officials, and leaders of industry and civic organizations. Perhaps not in numbers proportionate to their population, but change is always slow, even in a fast-moving nation such as ours.

It cheers me to think back to the time when I wrote my prison diary, when we were trying to break one more bone in the back of segregation, to know that our road to Parchman was part of the beginning of the changes that followed.

As I write this in 2018, however, even with laws that limit crimes and discrimination based on the color of one's skin, we all know that, though some of the horrifying injustices of the past are over, a staggering amount of racism still exists.

All these years later, the nation has not yet begun to confront the subtle, covert racism that is so pervasive, North and South. Indeed, it's out in the open again, revived and even encouraged in this era of Donald Trump.

It is heartbreaking to think that so many black people still live with the poverty heaved on their backs since the beginning of slavery. Black men are targeted by police and incarcerated in outrageous numbers for small crimes that the system lets whites get away with. Blacks live in exile within their own country, a country that celebrates its inclusiveness, but is still so perniciously exclusive.

No, this is not over.

What is needed now is for racism to be erased from the very soul of this nation. Now, as we near the 60th anniversary of the Freedom Rides, we must never turn back.

We still need to reaffirm, individually and as a country, the words spoken by Martin Luther King:

*Now is the time to lift our nation
from the quicksand of racial injustice to the solid
rock of brotherhood. Now is the time to make justice
a reality for all God's children.*

POSTSCRIPT: THEN AND NOW

When 2011 came, I went back to Jackson, Mississippi with my daughter Nina to take part in the 50th anniversary remembrance of the Freedom Rides. I knew there would be many people there whom I had never met, either because they weren't in jail when I was, or because they were men and were incarcerated in a separate cell block. But surely there would be some people with whom I had experienced so much and had become so emotionally attached to all those years ago. What were their lives like now? What had happened during all those intervening years? Whatever our separate paths, we had come to the reunion because we knew that our individual protests and the Movement we supported had truly bent history. We were going back where we were arrested, but this time without dread and without the sense that we had entered into a quite so alien, dangerous, and brutally segregated part of the country.

The first night we were honored at a celebratory dinner by none other than the city of Jackson. Local leaders—judges and municipal officials, both black and white—addressed us, and those who were black all made it very clear that, without the Civil Rights Movement, they could never have arrived in their present positions.

The next morning we all piled into buses for a tour of the mile posts in Mississippi's Civil Rights history. I caught sight of Wyatt Tee Walker, who had been the leader of my group of Freedom Riders. My memory of him as a slim and handsome young man probably no older than thirty-five gave way to the shock of seeing that he was now very old and in a wheelchair. I went to say hello, and realized that he was just as stunned to see how I had aged. Yes, fifty years had actually passed!

Nina and I boarded the bus and took seats next to each other. I loved being with her and being able to introduce her to just a bit of this part of my life. Nina is very outgoing and good with people, and in no time wonderful conversations were going on with Wyatt and others around us as the bus rolled along. At one point we discovered Sissy Leonard, the woman with the perfect skin who was on my 1961 bus ride. She was on the other side of the aisle and a couple of rows behind us, and I recognized her only by her name tag. I loved that little reunion.

When we passed by some of those old shacks by the roadside that I first saw in 1961 I was swept back as I remembered the dread and alarm I felt then. How amazing to again be in Mississippi, but without fear.

Our third stop was at the grocery store where in 1955 the chain of events began that ultimately led to the brutal murder of Emmett Till.

Later we visited the home and grave of Fannie Lou Hamer, a voting rights activist in the Civil Rights Movement and vice-chairman of the Mississippi Freedom Democratic Party, which she represented at the 1964 Democratic National Convention. Last of all we pulled through the entrance to Parchman State Penitentiary, just we as had in 1961. When we came to a stop, we were in front of the old brick maximum security unit. We got out of our seats, shook off our stiffness, exited the bus and were led through the same old path with the high wire fence to the entrance and into the building. I was catapulted into the past as I walked down the stairs I remembered so clearly, and into the cell blocks where we had been imprisoned. The guard accompanying us said that, although these cells were all empty at the moment, they now were used for Parchman's death row prisoners.

We were allowed to walk around freely, and in a kind of daze, I showed Nina my old cell and the iron cot where I had slept and where I had written my diary. It was exactly as I had always remembered it: the tiny space, the toilet in the back, and the small high windows across the hallway. I could almost hear the freedom songs we sang and feel our sustaining camaraderie, but now the place just seemed hollow, forlorn and very sad.

At lunchtime, uniformed prisoners served us a festive meal in a gray, bare walled function room. When we looked down at our plates, Nina and I burst out laughing at the small flyer placed in front of each person and proclaiming "Welcome Back Freedom Riders."

When I think about what all of us did during the Civil Rights Movement, I am proud and honored to have taken a small part in something that helped change the course of this country's history. However, it's impossible to escape awareness of the increasing bigotry and overt racism that are taking place now under Trump's leadership and policies. I hope this book might inspire some young people today to stand up, as we did in the sixties, to resist this disastrous trend.

Let's not let Martin Luther King Jr.'s dream die.

Acknowledgements

I want to thank the following people who helped and encouraged me while I was working on this book.

First of all, and most importantly come two people without whom I couldn't have finished this project. Many, many loving thanks to my husband Sib who spent so much time reading my first manuscripts, helping refresh my memory of some of the incidents we experienced, and making suggestions in places where my writing was a bit awkward. The second is Catherine Parnell, my editor, who I consider myself truly lucky to have found. Her support, suggestions, and guidance were far beyond anything I could have expected. Thank you, Catherine, from the bottom of my heart.

Thank you to Ann McArdle who helped me start writing, and to all the women in my writing group who propped me up and cheered me on: Pat Bridgeman, Yhanna Coffin, Dale Rosen, Kate Seidman, and Laurisa Sellers.

Thank you to Gail Falk for the materials she provided, the memories of Mississippi we shared, and the warmth of her friendship.

Thank you, Jan Weinshanker, for your supportive friendship and the many ways you encouraged me during the writing of this book.

Thank you to each one of my family and friends who, while I was working on this project, supported me in so many ways, including reading my manuscript and commenting on it.

Index of Images

Title Page: "Freedom Now" button photo courtesy of Judith Frieze Wright.

Page 5: Signs like this appeared all over the South.

Page 6: Photo of Emmett Till and his mother, Mamie Till Bradley Mobley, courtesy of the Collection of the Smithsonian National Museum of African American History and Culture, Gift of the Mamie Till Mobley family.

Page 7: 1963 Jackson, MS Woolworth Lunch Counter Sit-In photo courtesy of Fred Blackwell and the Wisconsin Historical Society.

Page 20: A group of Civil Rights workers share their strength by singing "We Shall Overcome" (1964). Photo courtesy of Civil Rights Movement Veterans (crmvet.org).

Page 24: Freedom Riders in a paddy wagon on their way to jail after being arrested in Jackson, Mississippi on June 2, 1961.

Page 25: Mug shot taken of Judith Frieze Wright, June 21, 1961. Photo Courtesy of the Archives and Records Services Division, Mississippi Department of Archives and History.

Page 28: A view of the entrance to Parchman State Penitentiary. This photo was taken in 2011 when many Freedom Riders returned for a 50th anniversary visit.

Page 32: Freedom Riders visited the maximum security unit at Parchman in 2011 on the 50th anniversary of the protest.

Page 34: Freedom Riders, including me, were taken to Parchman Prison's maximum security unit.

Page 39: Water fountain photo courtesy of Elliot Erwitt/ Magnum Photos.

Page 63: The COFO office Meridian, Mississippi (1963). Photo courtesy of Alan Reich and Civil Rights Movement Veterans (crmvet.org).

Page 70: Fannie Lee Chaney and son Ben at James Chaney's funeral. James Chaney, Andrew Goodman, and Michael Schwerner were abducted and murdered by the Klan in Neshoba County, Mississippi in June 1964 during the Civil Rights Movement.

Page 73: Andrew Goodman, James Chaney, and Michael Schwerner pictured on an FBI Missing poster displayed in 1964.

Page 75: Sheriff Rainey (right) and Deputy Sheriff Price at arraignment hearing in 1964 in Meridian, Mississippi.

Page 92: Luke Kabat surrounded by local teenagers outside the COFO office in Meridian, Mississippi. Photo courtesy of Bill Rodd.

Page 97: Memorial service for James Chaney, Andrew Goodman, and Michael Schwerner. Photo courtesy of Mark Levy Photos—Queens College/CUNY Civil Rights Archives.

Page 103: Johnnie Ruth watches while I show "Flap" Lanier how to play the harmonica.

Page 108: Posters similar to this, urging black people to vote, were seen in many towns across the Deep South during the Civil Rights struggle.

Page 113: Two adults discuss voter registration with a COFO volunteer in 1964. Photo courtesy of Ted Polumbaum.

Page 118: Practicing for the Lamar Hotel picket line inside the COFO office.

Page 136: Student protestors singing in front of the bus they would take to Mississippi to volunteer in COFO activities. Photo courtesy of Ted Polumbaum.

Page 142: John Doar with James Meredith, a twenty-nine-year-old veteran who decided in 1961 to apply to the then segregated University of Mississippi.

Page 157: Marchers being attacked by State Troopers and other white citizens on Bloody Sunday. On the ground to the right is John Lewis, later to become a United States Representative.

About the Author

Judith Frieze Wright was born in 1939 and is an artist living in Gloucester, Massachusetts. She became a Freedom Rider and was jailed in Mississippi in 1961. Later, in 1964, she spent a year in Meridian, Mississippi working with her husband Sib in the Civil Rights Movement. She is available for talks and can be contacted at judithfriezewright.com.

Made in the USA
Middletown, DE
22 May 2019